Introducing SEO

Your quick-start guide to effective
SEO practices

Aravind Shenoy
Anirudh Prabhu

Apress®

Introducing SEO: Your quick-start guide to effective SEO practices

Aravind Shenoy
Mumbai
Maharashtra, India

Anirudh Prabhu
Mumbai
India

ISBN-13 (pbk): 978-1-4842-1853-2
DOI 10.1007/978-1-4842-1854-9

ISBN-13 (electronic): 978-1-4842-1854-9

Library of Congress Control Number: 2016947491

Managing Director: Welmoed Spahr
Acquisitions Editor: Louise Corrigan
Development Editor: James Markham
Technical Reviewer: Richard Carter
Editorial Board: Steve Anglin, Pramila Balen, Laura Berendson, Aaron Black, Louise Corrigan, Jonathan Gennick, Celestin Suresh John, Nikhil Karkal, Robert Hutchinson, James Markham, Matthew Moodie, Ben Renow-Clarke, Natalie Pao, Gwenan Spearing
Coordinating Editor: Nancy Chen
Copy Editor: Tiffany Taylor
Compositor: SPi Global
Indexer: SPi Global
Cover Image: Courtesy of Freepik.com

Distributed to the book trade worldwide by Springer Science+Business Media New York, 233 Spring Street, 6th Floor, New York, NY 10013. Phone 1-800-SPRINGER, fax (201) 348-4505, e-mail orders-ny@springer-sbm.com, or visit www.springer.com. Apress Media, LLC is a California LLC and the sole member (owner) is Springer Science + Business Media Finance Inc (SSBM Finance Inc). SSBM Finance Inc is a **Delaware** corporation.

For information on translations, please e-mail rights@apress.com, or visit www.apress.com.

Apress and friends of ED books may be purchased in bulk for academic, corporate, or promotional use. eBook versions and licenses are also available for most titles. For more information, reference our Special Bulk Sales–eBook Licensing web page at www.apress.com/bulk-sales.

Any source code or other supplementary materials referenced by the author in this text is available to readers at www.apress.com. For detailed information about how to locate your book's source code, go to www.apress.com/source-code/.

Printed on acid-free paper

I dedicate this book to my late grandmother, Lilavati Kamath, and my sister, Aruna Nayak. I seriously appreciate their support in this rollercoaster ride called Life. Don't wanna say anything more, as it will spoil what I am trying to convey. Love you people.

—*Aravind Shenoy*

Contents at a Glance

Contents

About the Authors

Aravind Shenoy A senior technical writer by profession, Aravind's core interests are technical writing, content writing, content development, web design, and business analysis. He was born and raised in Mumbai and resides there. He is a music buff and loves listening to rock 'n' roll and rap. An engineering graduate from the Manipal Institute of Technology and an author of several books, he is a keen learner and believes there is always a steep learning curve, because Life is all about learning. In summary, as he quips, "The most important thing is to be happy"—he believes that is all that matters.

Anirudh Prabhu Anirudh a UI developer with more than seven years of experience. He specializes in HTML, CSS, JavaScript, jQuery, Sass, LESS, Twitter, and Bootstrap. Additionally, he has been associated with Packt and Apress books as a technical reviewer for several titles. He is the author of *Beginning CSS Preprocessors: with Sass, Compass, and Less* (Apress, 2015).

Anirudh has worked with coffeescript and angularJS. He's also been involved in building training material for HTML, CSS, and jQuery for twenty19 (`www.twenty19.com`), which is a portal for providing training for fresher/interns. In his free time, he enjoys listening to music and is also an avid photographer who likes taking unique photos.

About the Technical Reviewer

Richard Carter is a seasoned web designer and front-end developer based in the north of England. His interest in SEO comes from a desire to help clients and fully understand the implications in the ways websites are built and how they perform in search engines.

He lives in Newcastle upon Tyne and is the founder of the established UK web design agency Peacock Carter. Richard has worked with clients including the University of Edinburgh, NHS, City & Guilds, University College Dublin, and the Scottish government.

Acknowledgments

Thanks to the entire Apress team, especially Louise, Nancy, and James, for excellent support and patience while I was writing this book. A special thanks to the open source community where I started my journey. I really appreciate the book's technical reviewer, Richard, for the amazing feedback and input—thanks, Ric. Finally, I appreciate my coauthor, Anirudh, on this journey; thanks, dude.

—Aravind Shenoy

Introduction

Search engines are an integral part of the World Wide Web and help users search for almost anything on the internet. Google's search methodology paved the way for relevant search and was key to the rise of search engines on the web. Other search engines such as Yahoo!, Bing, Baidu, and Yandex have joined the fray as competition to Google.

Search engines were created to help users locate the most relevant information based on their search queries. Unfortunately, some sites began using underhand methods to get higher rankings in the search results. But this didn't go unnoticed, and search engines evolved so they could spot these discrepancies. The search engines also went through a paradigm shift and learned to recognize not only text but also interactive media. Industry experts estimate that Google uses more than 200 factors to rank websites in its search results.

You need to understand that users are the most critical aspect of search, because search engines were made to help them find information and content. Therefore, it is essential that you do not concentrate on fooling the search engines—doing so defeats the purpose of search. Your focus should be on user intent and user satisfaction, rather than using underhanded, manipulative techniques. As the engines continue to evolve, the focus has shifted to creating a streamlined user experience. After all, search is meant for users, and getting appropriate results is the primary purpose of the search engines. As the years go by, search protocols and ranking factors may change, but SEO and user experience will continue to work in conjunction with each other.

Another area to consider is enterprise search. Search engines continue to become smarter and can also cater to enterprise-search methodologies. And with social media and data science ruling the roost, you have a data mine waiting to be explored. All this can help give you insight into user preferences and experiences, leading to a major shift in the way people perceive SEO.

CHAPTER 1

▨ ▨ ▨

Introduction to SEO

When you explore aspects of managing websites, in addition to web design and user experience patterns, you come across the concept of *search engine optimization* (SEO): the science of improving a website's visibility across results from various search engines. If a website is not prominently visible in search results, it defeats the purpose of having a website in the first place. Therefore, it is extremely important to ensure that your website is easy for search engines to access.

Search engines such as Google, Yahoo!, and Bing help users find the content they are looking for. So, it is imperative that your website is visible on the search engine results page (SERP). For example, if you have a plumbing business offering services in Toronto, your site should rank high in the search engine rankings when users search for plumbers in Toronto on Google or any other search engine. Studies related to SEO suggest that more traffic usually results in more sales; therefore, traffic is one of the key components that determines revenue. In addition to increasing revenue, SEO can help with other goals such as reaching out to a larger audience or helping people access crucial information for a greater good.

Before delving into SEO methodology, you need to have a basic understanding of the following topics:

- What is SEO?

- Benefits of SEO

- Challenges in SEO

- Black-hat SEO vs. White-hat SEO

- On-page and Off-page SEO

This chapter discusses these in turn.

What Is SEO?

SEO is a methodology used to gain traffic by making your website visible in search engine results via organic or paid techniques. The term *organic* means using natural ways to enhance website visibility without using a pay-per-click service. There are many ways to implement SEO, such as using relevant keywords, quality content, and optimal multimedia content on your web pages.

© Aravind Shenoy and Anirudh Prabhu 2016
A. Shenoy and A. Prabhu, *Introducing SEO*, DOI 10.1007/978-1-4842-1854-9_1

In the past, people implemented underhand techniques (black-hat SEO) to gain website visibility. Google Search, Bing, and Yahoo! Search are the most prominent search engines used to locate information on the Web; and with these search engines getting smarter by the day, it is imperative that you use legitimate tactics to achieve natural visibility. Therefore, SEO can also be defined as the art or science of affecting website visibility in search results, ruling out using manipulative ways to trick the search engine. Google has laid out guidelines that must be adhered to, to ensure that site owners use appropriate tactics to implement SEO.

Benefits of SEO

SEO is not a cost but an investment that imparts results in the long term. You cannot expect a miracle to happen overnight—it takes weeks or even months to reach the top-of-the-results chart. There is no fixed way to accomplish this; however, a combination of several methods can help you achieve higher rankings in a calculative (and not manipulative) way.

The following are several advantages of implementing SEO in your web design projects:

- *Catering to a massive audience:* SEO is organic, and as your site goes up the rankings, you get more traffic. Studies related to various factors of SEO (link building, user-engaging content, and so on) indicate that sites visible in the first few pages of search engine results garner more traffic than the rest. For example, if a user wants to buy sneakers online, they usually click site links that appear on the first or second SERP without bothering to scroll through the rest; they do not want to spend too much of their valuable time and are looking for a quick resolution. Not only will traffic increase as a result of SEO, but the recommendations of users visiting your website will help you get more hits and attract new customers (a lot depends on the content or what's on offer— you learn about that in subsequent chapters). The reach and scope you achieve by implementing SEO leads to a larger target audience.

- *Permanent results:* When you use a pay-per-click approach, your site appears at the top of the SERP; however, the moment you stop paying for ads, the site will no longer be visible. On the other hand, SEO results are not dependent on ads, and with efficient maintenance, your site will appear at the top of the charts without having to advertise. You do not pay Google or advertising vendors to achieve the top spot on the SERP. (Note that at times, you may need the services of a digital marketing agency for various reasons, such as providing quality content on a regular basis or obtaining better online advertisement and exposure.)

- *Low cost of implementation:* In earlier days, marketing consultants advocated the use of brochures, ads, and television to advertise products. The amount of money spent on advertising was huge. Today, creating and hosting a website is not expensive. Hiring a digital marketing expert or using the services of a professional SEO organization can be a viable option, depending on your line of business or niche. In the long run, you can stabilize your site's position among the search results with minimum upkeep, resulting in a huge return on your investment for SEO implementation.

- *Data and analytics:* Earlier, data was used for monthly, annual, and sales reports by the top brass of an organization. However, data is used as a resourceful alternative with the advent of data science. Data helps you gain insight into customer preferences, marketing trends, and much more. You can get detailed analytics that help you determine game-changing factors for your business. For example, Google Analytics and Google Search Console let you gather data that can help you understand key aspects and drawbacks related to your site's visibility. You can also see conversions and bounce rates for the users visiting your website. For example, you can better judge the number of users actually buying something on your website vs. those who visited but did not make a transaction.

- *Staying ahead of the competition:* A plethora of free and commercial enterprise-grade SEO tools (for example, Google Analytics and Google Search Console) lets you see results and reports not only for your website but also for sites owned by your competitors. Therefore, you can compare your results with your competition. You receive statistics about various aspects of your competitors' business, such as the use of certain keywords, localization factors, and analytics. Thus, you can gain a better understanding of important competitive factors and steer clear of your competition.

- *Usability:* SEO and user experience go hand-in-hand. The future of SEO leans toward creating an enhanced user experience. For example, internal links on your website that point to relevant pages and content not only help search engines crawl your site but also result in easy navigation. Ultimately, SEO implementation should focus not on search engines but on the user's requirements and intent. Keeping this broad picture in mind, attracting users with engaging content and design is a recommended SEO trait that, in turn, aims at creating an awesome user experience. For example, Google advocates for mobile-friendly sites and ranks those sites higher, because mobile has become the de facto platform for business compared to desktop- or laptop-based sites.

- *Content marketing and branding:* Users tend to surf websites that are found among higher-ranked search results. Google encourages adherence to semantics and clean planning as opposed to underhanded techniques used by spammy websites. Therefore, if your page is among the top-ranked search results, it reflects a certain trust and credibility. In addition, the "content is king" paradigm encourages fresh content and engaging users, resulting in conversion optimization. As traffic increases, so will the credibility of your website. Therefore, you can ensure that the branding of the products on your site is apt, leading to better sales. This is why small- and medium-size enterprises are more focused on SEO implementation (compared to large-scale organizations, which have the funds to advertise through several channels) using localization and other techniques that result in brand awareness.

Challenges in SEO

The world of SEO has its hurdles. The following are various challenges you may come across when you implement SEO in your design projects:

- *Time constraints:* As mentioned earlier, people expect an SEO implementation to deliver quick results. In reality, it takes weeks or even months to see a positive result. A true SEO consultant always adheres to legitimate tactics and does not try to fool the search engines. Using devious tactics can help you gain results, but it will not be long before you are caught, resulting in penalties. Violations can cost you dearly. Some penalties are relatively lenient: your site is not featured in the top results as a result of being downgraded. But there are also severe penalties, including delisting your site from the search results (it depends on the severity of the violation).

- *Avoiding irrelevant, spammy content:* Content is king, as you will hear often in SEO training and tutorials. Well, content-driven websites usually fare well with SEO implementation, provided the content is engaging and relevant. Simply stuffing your content with keywords may not lead to good results. You need to understand user intent via their queries instead of focusing on what search engines like. For example, if your site advertises plumbing services in Toronto, then using irrelevant content such as smartphone reviews or vacations in Ibiza would be misleading. The focus of the content must not distract users. Users must receive the information they expect when they surf your website. Moreover, factors such as manipulating content, aggressive link building, and poor content may eventually prove detrimental. Search engines like fresh content. Therefore, if your content has not changed for a long time, or if you have used duplicate content from another website, your site will not appear in the top results.

- *Not including SEO while designing your website:* As mentioned earlier in the chapter, SEO and user experience (UX) go hand in hand. Implementing SEO in a project after the website has been designed may lead to discouraging results. While building the website, you need to consider factors important for SEO and UX design. For example, on an e-commerce website, it is imperative that the checkout facility is clearly visible, because some users just select an item and then want to check out. If the user cannot locate the checkout facility easily, it results in inefficient navigation, leading to a poor UX. Users will not visit a website again if they have difficulty navigating it.

- *Heavy-duty sites:* Cramming your website with as many features as possible or too much content can affect the UX significantly. Heavy-duty sites lead to excessive page-load times, and studies have suggested that users abandon searches if page-load times are not optimal. Less is more. Proper utilization of whitespace, efficient site architecture, and user-friendly design, along with relevant content, will streamline the UX, prompting users to return.

  An excellent example is the Google home page, www.google.com. There is a search box in the middle of the screen; users, on visiting the page, enter search terms in the box. Most users end up doing what Google expects them to do: search for information. There are no distractions on the page. This approach works because there is no bulk or clutter to waylay users when they visit the site.

- *Defective products:* Customers are the most important thing for businesses, and their feedback and recommendations are vital. If the quality of your products is not up to the mark, it is likely that users will not return, regardless of your website content. Apologies do not matter in the case of a flawed product or bad customer experience. Hence, the quality of your showcased products as well as efficient issue resolution are essential in generating user traffic to your website.

Black-Hat SEO vs. White-Hat SEO

Black-hat SEO can be defined as deceptive and underhand techniques used to scale up to higher rankings in search results. Most people tend to underestimate the potency of search engines in determining whether the techniques used are appropriate or deceitful. However, search engines are getting smarter by the day and can figure out whether you use improper tactics and strategies to fool them.

Black-hat SEO may get results in the short term, but eventually you will be penalized by the search engines. The following are a few ways these techniques are implemented:

- *Stuffing keywords into content:* Using massive numbers of keywords in your content may achieve short-term gains. However, if the keywords are not relevant to your content and are placed there just to fool the search engines, then eventually your site may be penalized. Remember, SEO is all about quality, not quantity; if your content is not good enough and is packed with keywords, your site may not be visible in the top search results because you are being penalized by the search engines.

- *Link farming:* Buying links is never fruitful, because the search engines will know you are manipulating them. Using inappropriate links pointing to your website is detrimental because the search engines will realize that the links have no relevance and are not authentic. For example, suppose your site offers plumbing services to people in Florida. If several links on a travel website in Toronto point to your site, it doesn't make sense: travel services are in no way connected to plumbing services. Using such deceptive techniques can have long-term consequences and may even result in your site being delisted from search results.

- *Doorway pages and cloaking: Doorway pages* are used to gain high rankings in search results in a deceitful manner. These pages contain keywords and phrases that are picked up by search-engine bots and crawlers. Once you click to access the page, you are redirected to the actual page that the site owners want you to visit. *Cloaking* is a mechanism that renders a page visible to search engines but not website users. This short-sighted technique can prove detrimental in the long run. Google has announced penalties for using doorways, deceptive redirects, and cloaking.

There is much more to black-hat SEO, which you learn about in later chapters.

White-hat SEO is the opposite of black-hat SEO and is focused on using optimal, organic tactics to help your site rank higher in search results. Usually it means adhering to the guidelines provided by the search engines and playing by the rules. Factors such as quality link building, user-engaging content, and optimal performance are some of the white-hat SEO strategies used by SEO consultants to streamline accessibility and visibility in search rankings. In short, you need to focus on user intent rather than try to fool the search engines.

On-Page and Off-Page SEO

SEO methodology involves many factors, and no site can claim to use all of them at the same time. Basically, these factors are divided into two types:

- On-page SEO (or on-site SEO)
- Off-page SEO (or off-site SEO)

On-page SEO consists of factors that are in your area of control, including your code. It includes metatags and metadescriptions, headings, title tags, internal links within the site, site maps, page-load time, semantics, and ease of navigation, to mention a few (see Figure 1-1). On-page SEO generally focuses on efficient presentation of content to website users. Adhering to semantics and optimal web page structure are imperative for a site's success: they result in a site that is systematic and organized and that provides better readability not only for users but also for indexing by search-engine crawlers.

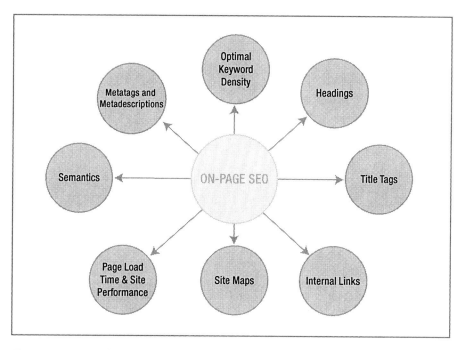

Figure 1-1. *On-page SEO factors*

Off-page SEO factors include things that are not dependent on the code or are not under your control. These include forum postings, social media marketing, social bookmarking, blogs, and RSS feeds (see Figure 1-2). Off-page SEO is essential in the long term as you create a community for your content. Social networking is a key factor for creating a positive online reputation, and off-page SEO lends significant trust and credibility if you play by the rules.

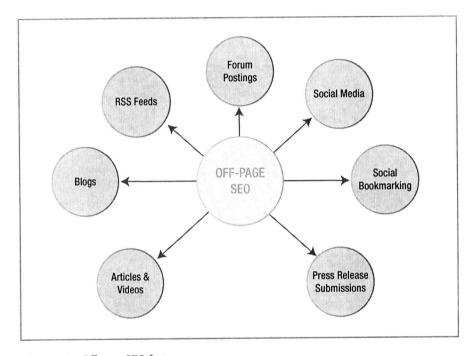

Figure 1-2. Off-page SEO factors

Summary

This chapter looked at the concept of SEO and the advantages associated with incorporating SEO in your design project. You now understand the challenges involved in SEO implementation and the constraints associated with it. You learned about the types of SEO—black-hat SEO vs. white-hat SEO—as well as on-page and off-page SEO factors. The next chapter looks at search engines and their components, including their relevance to SEO methodology.

CHAPTER 2

Search Engines

A *search engine* is a tool that searches the Web for websites relevant to real-time queries entered by users. Depending on the search string, search engines return results, which are called search engine results page (SERPs). Usually the engines get it right and display the most relevant results. There are no fixed rules used by the search engines to display accurate results.

Spiders or *crawlers* are robots that search for and index website content. The most popular search engines are Google, Yahoo!, and Bing. Search engines can determine the most relevant web pages because the companies have developed algorithms for the search process. Nowadays, quality link building, fresh and intuitive content, and streamlined navigation are the core factors that determine which websites get priority at the top of the search results. There are other factors, such as popularity of the website, relevance of the content, and use of interactive media, although the exact logic used to obtain results is a business secret. SEO is moving toward a user experience (UX) paradigm, and search engines are constantly evolving and getting smarter by the day.

Evolution of Search Engines

The concept of a search engine was laid out a long time ago. In 1990, the first search engine was released. The founders named it Archie (*archive* without a *v*). The following year, Veronica and Jughead were released. 1993 saw the launch of Excite and World Wide Web Wanderer. In the same year, Aliweb and Primitive Web Search were launched. Infoseek was a venture where webmasters could submit their pages in a real-time scenario. However, the game changer was AltaVista: it was the first engine that had unlimited bandwidth and could understand natural-language queries. The following years saw the launch of WebCrawler, Yahoo! Web Directory, Lycos, LookSmart, and Inktomi.

Google founders Larry Page and Sergey Brin created the BackRub search engine, which focused on backlinks. Unlike other search engines, which focused on keyword relevance, the Page Rank algorithm in BackRub used backlinks to determine higher rankings in search results. Later, Page and Brin changed the name of the search engine to Google and paved the way for the search engine revolution.

In 1997, the search engine Ask Jeeves was launched; unlike Google, it used human editors to analyze and sort search queries. However, it depended on the principle of keyword relevance, and its business was changed from a web search engine to a question-and-answer site in 2010. Yahoo! Search depended on Inktomi, an OEM search engine, until 2002.

© Aravind Shenoy and Anirudh Prabhu 2016
A. Shenoy and A. Prabhu, *Introducing SEO*, DOI 10.1007/978-1-4842-1854-9_2

After acquiring other search utilities such as AltaVista and Overture, Yahoo! developed its own web-spider-based engine. MSN, a web portal created by Microsoft, launched MSN Search in 1999. It evolved into Live Search and was later rebranded as Bing. Figure 2-1 shows the timeline and search engines launched from 1990 to the present.

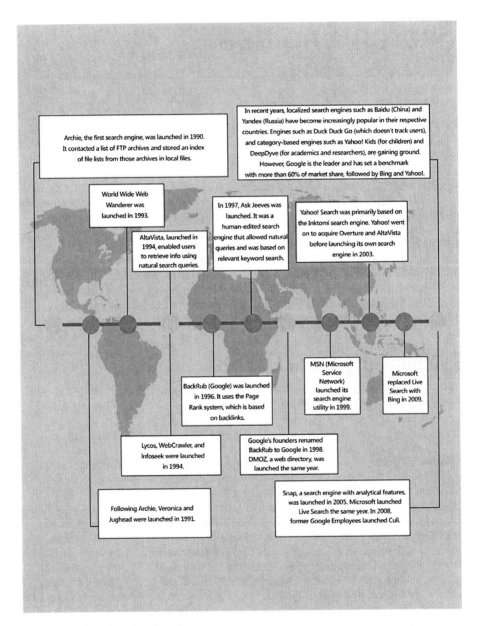

Figure 2-1. Search engine timeline

Google, with its highly accurate results, is currently the most sought-after search engine and is preferred by the vast majority of users, compared to Bing and Yahoo!. Google's innovative search capabilities and market penetration make it the leader in the search engine industry.

At the time of writing, you can find statistics for the net market share of various search engines on both desktop and mobile platforms at `www.netmarketshare.com/search-engine-market-share.aspx?qprid=4`. (Note that it is impossible to determine exact results, because search-engine evolution, innovation, user perception, and protocols change every day. Thus, these statistics are approximate.) You can filter the results based on browser, operating system, and device type. For example, Figure 2-2 shows the statistics for the net market share of desktop devices. You can clearly see the impact of Google: it is the search engine of choice on desktop devices, although other search engines are gaining ground.

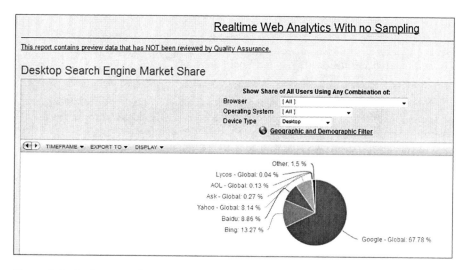

Figure 2-2. *Desktop search engine market share*

Figure 2-3 shows the statistics for the net market share of mobile devices. Google is also predominantly the search engine of choice for users on the mobile/tablet platform.

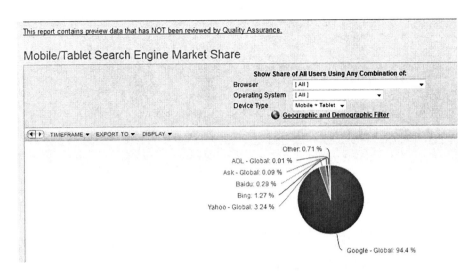

Figure 2-3. *Mobile/Tablet search engine market share*

Apart from the big three, search engines such as Baidu (China), Yandex (Russia), and Naver (South Korea) are causing a shift in user preferences when localization factors are taken into consideration.

The need to do deep web searching for content that is not easily accessible has led to the evolution of initiatives such as DeepDyve and Yippy, which cater to niche interests. And with users keen on privacy, search engines such as Duck Duck Go (which avoids spammy sites and doesn't track users' search history) have come into prominence.

The future of search engines is leaning toward effective enterprise search focused on increasing productivity across organizations. Search engines are becoming more intuitive and category-based. A paradigm shift is coming, where search engines will be used not only for personal use but also for professional verticals. For example, Indeed is a job portal. These special search engines are typically known as *vertical search engines* and cater to a specific audience; they help users locate information that usually is not available in the results of traditional search engines. Web portals are baked-in with search engines and directory approaches and increasingly lean toward creating a satisfying user experience. Another new aspect is voice search, where search engines will become an intelligent ecosystem based on user intent. As people's needs develop and search engines evolve, and machine learning taking data science to a new level, the future looks to be more personal and enterprise-based, which will help resolve the various associated complexities with relative ease.

Search Engine Processes and Components

Modern search engines perform the following processes:

- Web crawling
- Indexing
- Searching

This section presents an overview of each of these before you move on to understanding how a search engine operates.

Web Crawling

Web crawlers or *web spiders* are internet bots that help search engines update their content or index of the web content of various websites. They visit websites on a list of URLs (also called *seeds*) and copy all the hyperlinks on those sites. Due to the vast amount of content available on the Web, crawlers do not usually scan everything on a web page; rather, they download portions of web pages and usually target pages that are popular, relevant, and have quality links. Some spiders normalize the URLs and store them in a predefined format to avoid duplicate content. Because SEO prioritizes content that is fresh and updated frequently, some crawlers visit pages where content is updated on a regular basis. Other crawlers are defined such that they revisit all pages regardless of changes in content. It depends on the way the algorithms are written. If a crawler is archiving websites, it preserves web pages as snapshots or cached copies.

Crawlers identify themselves to web servers. This identification process is required, and website administrators can provide complete or limited access by defining a `robots.txt` file that educates the web server about pages that can be indexed as well as pages that should not be accessed. For example, the home page of a website may be accessible for indexing, but pages involved in transactions—such as payment gateway pages—are not, because they contain sensitive information. Checkout pages also are not indexed, because they do not contain relevant keyword or phrase content, compared to category/product pages.

If a server receives continuous requests, it can get caught in a *spider trap*. In that case, the administrators can tell the crawler's parents to stop the loops. Administrators can also estimate which web pages are being indexed and streamline the SEO properties of those web pages.

Googlebot (used by Google), BingBot (used by Bing and Yahoo!), and Sphinx (an open source, free search crawler written in C++) are some of popular crawlers indexing the web for their respective search engines. Figure 2-4 shows the basic functional flow of a web crawler.

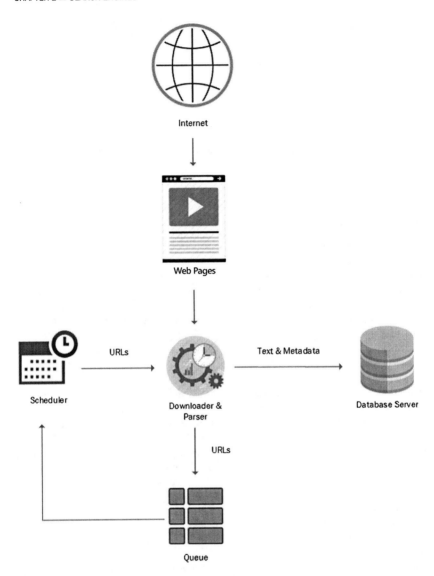

Figure 2-4. *Structural schema of a web crawler*

Indexing

Indexing methodologies vary from engine to engine. Search-engine owners do not disclose what types of algorithms are used to facilitate information retrieval using indexing. Usually, sorting is done by using forward and inverted indexes. *Forward indexing* involves storing a list of words for each document, following an asynchronous system-processing methodology; that is, a *forward index* is a list of web pages and which words appear on those web pages. On the other hand, *inverted indexing* involves locating documents that contain the words in a user query; an *inverted index* is a list of words and which web pages those words appear on. Forward and inverted indexing are used for different purposes. For example, in forward indexing, search-engine spiders crawl the Web and build a list of web pages and the words that appear on each page. But in inverted indexing, a user enters a query, and the search engine identifies web pages linked to the words in the query.

During indexing, search engines find web pages and collect, parse, and store data so that users can retrieve information quickly and effectively. Imagine a search engine searching the complete content of every web page without indexing—given the huge volume of data on the Web, even a simple search would take hours. Indexes help reduce the time significantly; you can retrieve information in milliseconds.

Forward indexing and inverted indexing are also used in conjunction. During forward indexing, you can store all the words in a document. This leads to asynchronous processing and hence avoids bottlenecks (which are an issue in inverted indexes). Then you can create an inverted index by sorting the words in the forward index, to streamline the full-text search process.

Information such as tags, attributes, and image alt attributes are stored during indexing. Even different media types such as graphics and video can be searchable, depending on the algorithms written for indexing purposes.

Search Queries

A user enters a relevant word or a string of words to get information. You can use plain text to start the retrieval process. What the user enters in the search box is called a *search query*. This section examines the common types of search queries: navigation, informational, and transactional.

Navigational Search Queries

These types of queries have predetermined results, because users already know the website they want to access. Figure 2-5 shows an example: the user has typed **Yahoo** in the search box and wants to access the Yahoo! website. Because the user already knows the destination to be accessed, this falls under the heading of a navigational query.

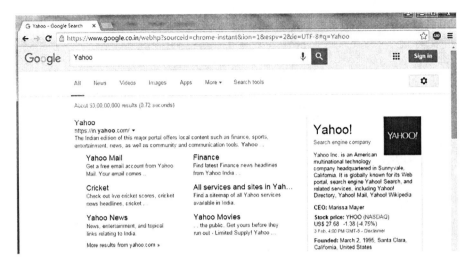

Figure 2-5. *Navigational search query*

Informational Search Queries

Informational search queries involve finding information about a broad topic and are more generic in nature. Users generally type in real-time words to research or expand their knowledge about a topic.

In Figure 2-6, the user has entered a query about how to troubleshoot a router. They want information about a broad topic—the query is generic and is not limited to a specific router such as D-Link or Cisco.

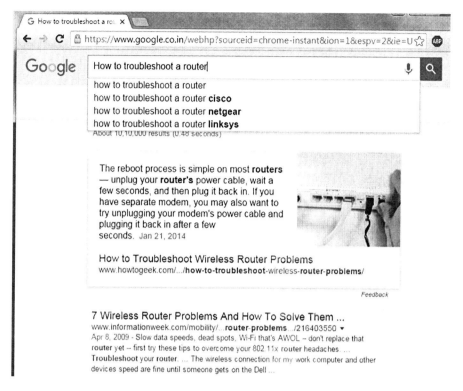

***Figure 2-6.** Informational search query*

Transactional Search Queries

In this type of query, the user's intent is focused on a transaction, which may be generic or specific. In Figure 2-7, the user wants to check the price of Nike shoes on online shopping portals (this example uses Bing as the search engine). The user knows the brand of shoes they want to buy, and in this case the search is related to making a purchase. However, not all transactional search queries are purchase-based; they can also involve the user wanting to take some sort of action, such as signing up for a portal.

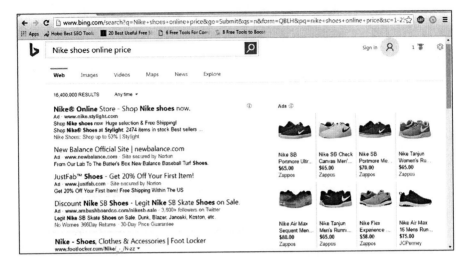

Figure 2-7. *Transactional search query*

How Search Engines Work

The previous sections looked at the components and processes related to search engines. This section puts the pieces together so that you understand how a search engine works.

A search-engine spider visits a website and accesses the `robots.txt` file to learn which pages of the site are accessible. On gaining access, it sends information about the content to be indexed: this may be hypertext, headings, or title tags, depending on the markup and page content. The spider or bot then turns the information into an *index*: a list of terms and the web pages containing those terms.

Web crawlers are constantly updating their index as they search for fresh information. Figure 2-8 shows the functional flow of bots or spiders accessing web pages, and then creating and storing indexes along with relevant data on the database server.

Figure 2-8. *Functional flow for bots accessing web pages and storing indexes and data*

When users enter real-time words in a search box to retrieve information, the index containing those terms and their associated websites is accessed. Algorithms (lengthy mathematical equations) configured for ranking the results come into play, and accurate results are displayed on *search engine result pages* (SERPs). The algorithms determine which sites are ranked higher by assigning values to web pages depending on various factors: fresh, engaging content; localization; metadata; semantics; and fonts displaying prominence, to name a few. With search engines getting smarter by the day, the algorithms keep changing and evolving to deliver accurate results in a matter of milliseconds. Figure 2-9 shows how a search query ends up in SERPs.

| Users | Search engine database server | Web Page |

Figure 2-9. *User search queries result in SERPs*

Searches can also use filters. You can customize a search by using filters that help you get the most relevant information. You can also classify results by using filters according to the categories or media types.

Figure 2-10 shows category filters such as News, Images, and Maps that help users search by media type. In addition, search filters such as Country, Date, and Time filter results further. By being more specific, you can obtain meaningful results and do content-based or concept-based searching.

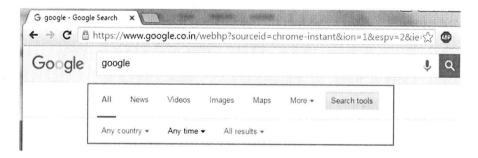

Figure 2-10. *Google search filters*

Web Directories

Not every site is highly ranked in search results, due to heavy volume and competition on the Web. Your site also may not rank as high if your advertising budget is small compared that of the heavyweights. It is also becoming difficult for local websites to achieve higher rankings, because most of the sites are optimized to gain maximum visibility. In addition, most users use Google, Yahoo!, or Bing (or, in China, Baidu), and not every site can compete with its rivals to rank higher in those engines' search results, given the limited options. You need to gauge the alternatives to gain better visibility and increase accessibility to your site.

Prior to the creation of search engines, web directories were the de facto medium for businesses to reach out to the masses. A web directory contains a collection of links to websites arranged alphabetically or categorized by niche. For example, a website for a plumbing business appears in the Plumbing category, if such a category exists. Most web directories are manually edited, meaning humans sort and enter links based on the categories. Links to your site work as backlinks and help streamline the site's accessibility to crawlers.

For example, DMOZ is a comprehensive, human-edited web directory maintained by voluntary editors and reviewers. It is the default, widely used web catalogue. Some web directories are free, whereas others are commercial. Best of the Web Directory (https://botw.org/) is an example of a paid directory service. A listing in a popular online directory increases your site's visibility significantly, thereby helping you garner more traffic. With high-quality links and an increase in reliable, relevant traffic, your website may receive a fair amount of exposure. Moreover, by appearing in an optimal online directory, your website reflects credibility, which is a boon for brick-and-mortar businesses.

Summary

This chapter explored the various components involved in search engines and gave you a basic idea of their functionality. You looked at various types of queries and learned about web directories. In addition to Google, Yahoo!, and Bing, you can use special search engines that are topical and help you search niche information belonging to a specific category.

CHAPTER 3

Ranking in SEO

A few years ago, there was certain predictability in understanding the factors that let to a site being ranked higher in search results. However, many professionals used black-hat SEO techniques (such as link farming and stuffing pages with keywords) to gain higher rankings. Using underhanded techniques may have elevated sites in the rankings initially, but the sites were penalized later by the search engines. The deceptive techniques were rank-specific and did not take website users or customers into consideration.

Over time, search engines became more efficient at judging sites based on user intent and weeding out sites that were using deceit to rank higher on search engine result pages (SERPs). Today you cannot get away with spamming the search engines—Google and the others have become adept at knowing which sites are adhering to their guidelines.

Studies suggest that search engines consider more than 250 factors when ranking sites. Although the exact attributes that result in better rankings are not specified (they are a business secret), the fundamentals have shifted toward an enhanced user experience (UX) and providing meaningful content. "Content is king" is an adage you may have heard a million times, but the scenario has changed: "*Relevant* content is king" is the new mantra and is an apt motivator toward a streamlined UX. You should focus on user intent and user satisfaction rather than design sites for the search engines.

SEO is an amalgam of relevance and best practices designed to help users find information related to their queries. This chapter looks at on-page, on-site, and off-page SEO factors that form the crux of SEO.

On-Page SEO

On-page optimization is related to factors controlled by you or your code that have an effect on your site's rankings in search results. To create an optimal experience, you need to focus on the following page-optimization factors (see Figure 3-1):

- Title tags

- Meta keywords and meta descriptions

- Headings

- Engaging content

© Aravind Shenoy and Anirudh Prabhu 2016
A. Shenoy and A. Prabhu, *Introducing SEO*, DOI 10.1007/978-1-4842-1854-9_3

- Image optimization
- Interactive media
- Outbound and internal links

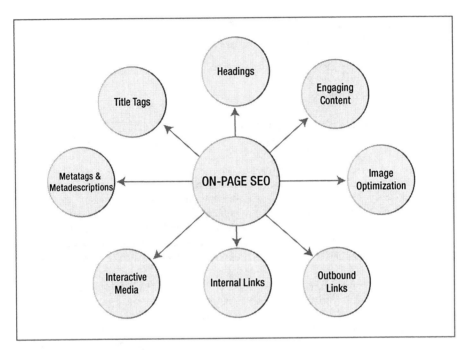

Figure 3-1. *On-page SEO*

Title Tag Optimization

In a page's HTML code, the <title> tag gives an indication of the page content. (You can find the words used between the `<title>` tags by viewing the page source in Firefox; the method varies depending on the browser.) Figure 3-2 shows the location of a title on a web page as well as where it can be located in the code.

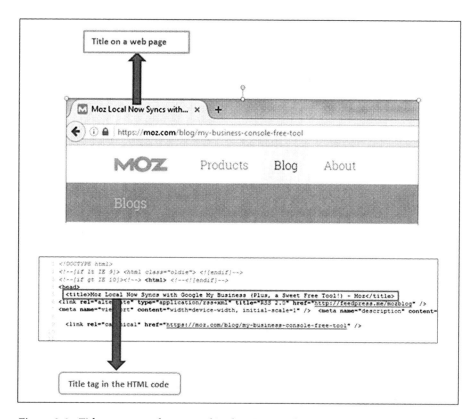

Figure 3-2. *Title tag on a web page and in the HTML code*

Search engines display the page title as the title of the search snippet link on SERPs. However, the title of a search snippet may also depend on the search query.

Figure 3-3 shows the search results for a query about a Zurb Foundation 6 book in Google Search in the Chrome browser. This example uses **zurb foundation 6 book amazon** as the search query; therefore, in the highlighted box in the search results, you can see the website search snippet for that book on Amazon.

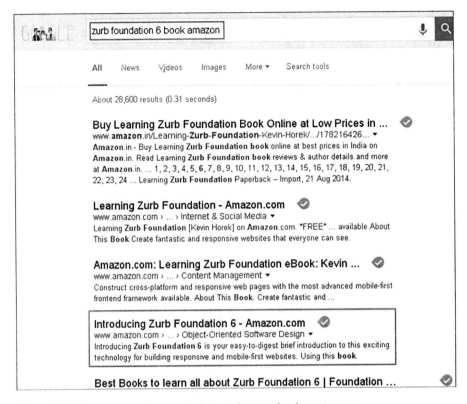

Figure 3-3. Search query about a Zurb Foundation 6 book on Amazon

Now let's change the search query to **Introducing Zurb Foundation 6 Aravind**. The results list the same website, but the title of the search snippet is different (see Figure 3-4).

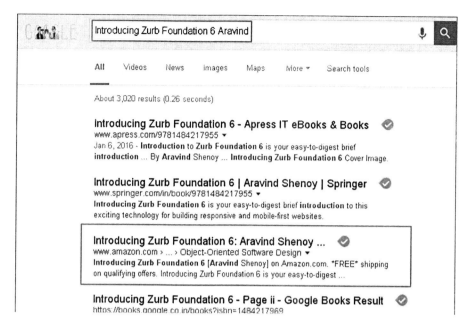

Figure 3-4. *The same website displays a different title for the altered search query*

Over time, depending on the links and their age, a search snippet may change dynamically for the same result. Thus there is no fixed rule for how to create a page title. The title may also vary depending on the platform—especially for responsive websites on small, medium, and large screens.

Do not stuff keywords into a page title, because Google may penalize your site for manipulating the natural search process. Also avoid using irrelevant phrases or a single keyword in the page title. Your page title should educate users about the page content and thus must be relevant and related to the page content. Single keywords face a lot of competition, because thousands of websites use the same keyword; it is better to use *long-tail terms,* which may be a mix of keywords and related phrases. Also keep in mind that each page on the website should have a unique title.

The best practice, according to SEO experts, is to use a phrase containing relevant words (say, 8–11 words) with at most 55–65 characters. This makes sense, because extremely long phrases will not work well on mobile devices where space is a constraint. Titles must be precise and concise, and can use a mix of uppercase and lowercase characters. Avoid commonly used titles or duplicate content, because search engines display a preference for unique titles. Google Search prefers function over form, so it is a best practice to use a simple, unique title rather than a sensational, irrelevant title. You should understand and consider user intent rather than looking at titles from a search engine point of view.

Meta Keywords and Meta Descriptions

Recently, Google confirmed that it doesn't consider meta keywords and descriptions as ranking factors. Nevertheless, meta keywords and meta descriptions are cached, so it would not be a best practice to ignore them. Although they are not consequential in determining search engine results, meta descriptions can be an excellent way of advertising; they may or may not be displayed in the search results.

Figure 3-5 provides an example of a meta description. It is a good practice to limit the meta description to 155–170 characters. It provides a preview of the content or information on that page and should contain the gist of the entire page. If the description is apt, informative, and meets the needs of the user, it may work like free advertising: the user may be compelled to click that site link to view the content.

Figure 3-5. *Meta description*

The meta description must be unique for each page on a website, like the page title. Avoid stuffing the description with keywords, and remove all special characters. Using multiple meta keywords can have a negative influence on search engines.

The meta robots attribute is increasingly being used by web designers. It tells crawlers whether the page should be displayed in SERPs (index/noindex) or whether you should depend on the links on the page (follow/nofollow).

Heading Tags (h1, h2, h3, h4, h5, and h6)

Heading tags are an important on-page factor. The <h1> (heading 1) tag is crucial and must be relevant to the topic discussed on the web page. It educates readers about the topic on that page. Instead of filling a page with clutter, it is a good practice to stick to a single topic; the heading 1 tag is imperative, because it indicates the page's topic. Use relevant words in the heading to help users and also spiders understand the page's content. Google adheres to text semantics and emphasizes its use for better results.

Avoid skipping heading levels on a web page. <h1> should be followed by <h2>, which in turn may have a <h3>, and so on. You may have multiple <h2> tags or subsequent tags, if needed. Your web page must display a systematic pattern or consistency. If the formatting or styling of the headings is not to your liking, you can use CSS styling to alter it.

Include keywords, but do not repeat them in the heading. Keywords used at the beginning of a heading yield better results. Avoid spamming or using irrelevant words in headings, because doing so may have a negative effect.

Engaging Content

Using meaningful and pertinent content in the body section of the site is vital. Relevant content is king. The content should not be irrelevant or stuffed with keywords—the search engines may penalize you for it. However, you can use keywords or close variations of them twice or three times on a page in a logical way. The content should be informative and engage the user, encouraging them to return to check out the site regularly. It is a good practice to update the content (such as technology topics) at least every six months, because Google has a penchant for updated or fresh content. (News channel sites update their content on a daily basis. Here, we are referring to product pages or informative sites, and updating or adding content for a product or topic.) Blogs must be updated on a regular basis. Use interactive media such as images, videos, and audio files on your web pages; they are intuitive and engage users, and may make the site more popular. Always spell-check and proofread your content, because incorrect grammar or spelling errors can reflect negatively on your site.

In addition to having meaningful content, quantity of content matters. You cannot use a keywords 3 times in 140 characters—that is keyword stuffing. In-depth, detail-oriented, relevant content helps you space out keywords evenly. It also helps users to understand the logic of the content, especially if the topic is informative and educates the user significantly. However, do not use 2,000 words just to fill the page; low-quality content results in bad UX. Remember, less is more, because quality is more important than quantity—function over form.

Bounce rate reflects the number of users who visit a web page and then leave. It doesn't matter how much time they spend on the page; it focuses on whether users leave the site after viewing just one page. Low-quality content results in higher bounce rates and will eventually affect the site's visibility.

Do not copy content from another website or use boilerplate content. Google search engines have been known to penalize sites that use duplicate content. Focus on user satisfaction and not on fooling the search engines. At times there are legitimate reasons for duplicate content: for example, an e-commerce site will have the same content on different pages with different URLs due to filters such as size, color, and price. Some websites have the same content on different web pages with the prefixes HTTP and HTTPS; although the rest of the URLs are the same, the prefixes mean they are treated as separate pages. Sometimes the watered-down mobile version of a website has the same content as the desktop version, resulting in duplication. Localization may also be a factor: for example, www.google.com may appear as as www.google.co.in for India. The content may be the same, but the URLS are different. In such cases, search engines may not allocate as high a ranking, because two different URLs have the same or similar content.

You can resolve these issues by using either a canonical tag or a 301 direct. A *301 redirect* is a permanent redirect from one URL to another that helps users reach the new address. It can also be used for "404 Page not found" errors where content has been moved to a different web page.

A canonical *tag* is an alternative where you apply a `rel=canonical` attribute to tell search engines the original or preferred content and the URL to be indexed for display in SERPs. For example, suppose these two websites have the same content: `http://example97653.com` and `http://example234.com/seo12345/56473`. The first URL is the original, getting the maximum number of hits. You want this site address to be indexed. To implement the canonical tag, you go the HTML code for the second URL and, in the `<head>` element, add the following:

```
<link rel="canonical" href="http://example97653.com"/>
```

You use the `canonical` attribute in the head element of the HTML markup for the URL containing the duplicate content and link it to the original or preferred URL.

Image Optimization and Interactive Media

Earlier SEO was text-based, but this has changed significantly. You should use interactive media such as audio, video, images, and infographics to connect with your users. Use captions and alternate text for media, and build relevant content around these media. You can use a single key phrase in the `alt` text if it is relevant to that image. You can interchange images based on the screen size, with heavy-duty images for desktop sites and lightweight images for mobile sites. Try to limit the image file size to less than 80–90 KB for optimal page-loading time. Use PNG or JPEG image formats wherever possible, because they are robust and have more visual properties. Using thumbnails and different angles for a product can be very handy, especially on e-commerce sites.

Using videos explaining a product or marketing a certain entity is a good practice. Google owns YouTube, and it can be a game-changing means of branding your product. Infographics are an excellent way to provide information or create timelines with relevant content.

Outbound and Internal Links

Internal links are a key feature of SEO. These are links on web pages that point to another page in the site or domain. SEO-related research suggests that no page on your website should be more than three clicks from the home page, meaning all pages should be easily accessible. You can use relevant anchor text to point to different pages on your site. *Breadcrumbs* are an efficient way to provide site navigation using links. Having a good link structure makes it easy for search engines to crawl your entire website, and easy accessibility also leads to an awesome UX.

Outbound links point to another domain or site. They are a good feature for informative or niche topics. Sometimes a page includes jargon or topic-specific terms; instead of wasting time explaining supplementary information on the page, you can use URLs or anchor text as outbound links to locations that explain the information in depth. SEO experts tend to doubt the content found on Wikipedia, but it is actually an excellent source of free, relevant, detail-oriented information. For example, suppose you are explaining web servers, and you use the word *server* in your content. Instead of explaining what a server is, you can use the word as anchor text to link to a wiki site that explains the meaning and use of servers. Linking specific terms to wiki sites such as Wikipedia and

Webopedia may boost your SEO process. Not only is doing so relevant, but it also lends a certain amount of trust and credibility to your site. You can use outbound links to social media sites or blogs to help reach out to a larger audience. Just be sure you do not link to spammy or illegal sites—doing so may negate your SEO efforts, because search engines will penalize your site. Also do not link to sites that are not relevant to the topic, because two-way linking or link farming can be detrimental. (You learn more about links in Chapter 8.)

On-Site SEO

Whereas on-page SEO is relevant to individual pages, on-site features affect your SEO process on the website as a whole. This section explains the following (see Figure 3-6):

- URL optimization

- Site maps

- Domain trust

- Localization

- Mobile site optimization and responsive websites

- Site-loading speed or page-load time

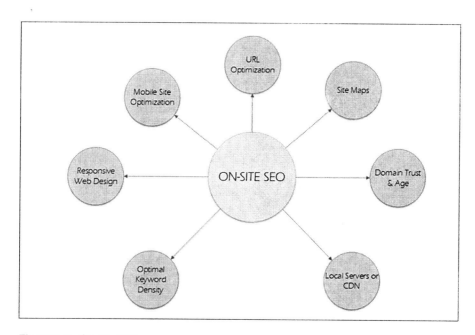

Figure 3-6. *On-site SEO*

URL Optimization

URLs play an important role in SEO, and you need to plan holistically for making your URLs as SEO-friendly as possible. Each URL should be human-readable and not consist of a bunch of special characters or numbers mixed with words. It should be meaningful and should reflect what the site is about. For example, `https://www.searchenginejournal.com` is meaningful because it tells readers that the site offers a comprehensive array of topics and guides related to SEO. Using hyphens (-) instead of underscores is a good practice recommended by Google. SEO experts advocate the use of `canonical` tags or 301 redirects for duplicate pages or pages with similar content; otherwise the value of the content may be negated, because as ranking signals may split it across the multiple URLs. For "404 Page not found" errors, you need to use 301 redirects to guide users to a working URL for that content.

Using a `robots.txt` file helps inform search engines about pages to be ignored while crawling the site. For example, a Contact Us page or About Us page may be useful if users need to access or buy a product or need help from the customer service department. However, a normal user may not find the Disclaimers page important and hardly skim such pages. So, it is essential to educate crawlers about which pages need to be indexed for SEO processes. You can also indicate broken links and 404 pages in the `robots.txt` file.

SEO experts advocate the user of a *favicon* on the title bar next to the URL, because it lends credibility and helps with effective branding. It helps users recognize your site and improves trustworthiness significantly. Although there are no direct benefits from favicons from a SEO perspective, they enhance usability. Bookmarks in the Google Chrome browser send out signals to the Google search engine that maps bookmarks for sites on the Web. This it is not a major factor, but it certainly helps from a user perspective. Figure 3-7 shows the favicon for LinkedIn:

Figure 3-7. *The LinkedIn favicon makes it easy to recognize the website and lends a trust factor to the brand*

Site Maps

There are two types of site maps: XML site maps, which are tailored to search engines; and HTML site maps, which are directed toward users. An XML site map contains a machine-readable list of pages on your site that you want search engines to index for SEO purposes. It contains information for crawlers such as the last update, its relevance or importance, alterations, and related data. XML site maps are domain-related and help spiders perform a deep search of web pages. For example, issues such as broken links or a lack of internal linking can be crucial factors that may result in crawlers not being able to index pages. There is no guarantee that a site map will cause crawlers to index all of your website's pages; however, it will significantly help with accessibility, because search engines can digest such data easily.

An HTML site map is tailored to your website's users and helps users locate different pages. All categories and products can be listed explicitly. It streamlines the user experience by making users familiar with your website and provides better semantics. UX is a vital aspect of SEO, so it is a good practice to include both XML and HTML site maps in your process. Make sure your XML site maps for search engines are exhaustive; on the other hand, HTML site maps should be more concise so users can navigate them more easily.

Domain Trust and Local Domains

Your domain can be a key ranking factor because it creates trust and credibility for site users. Studies suggest that domains registered for two years or longer were considered more trustworthy than new domains. Use the .com domain extension, because it is more common than .org and other extensions. *Domain localization*—catering to a specific country or city—may prove to be a game changer. For example, .co.uk caters to the United Kingdom and is more specific to users in that region and those with business links to the UK. Choosing a domain with a good reputation is helpful. If the domain has been assessed some kind of penalty, it can be detrimental to your business due to lack of credibility.

Using keywords in a domain name may be useful; however, given all the keywords that have already been used by websites, you may not be able to have the domain name of your choice.

Your domain name is crucial, because it indicates what your site is all about. Opt for a simpler, unique, relevant domain name rather than a sensational name, to help users connect with your site. You can use an online dictionary to check words related to your service or product. You can also use a combination of two or three words, such as DealOn, ScoutMob, or HomeRun. You can even think outside of the box and come up with something really creative, such as Reddit, Google, and Yelp, to name a few. Again, focus on your prospective customers and come up with something catchy and easy to spell that they can relate to; for example, if you search for plumbers or plumbing in Miami, you see http://www.miami-plumbers.com/ in the results. The name conveys that this is a plumbing business and the region (Miami) where they provide plumbing services.

Mobile Site Optimization and Responsive Websites

The digital marketing era has seen the rise of smartphones as the preferred option for online purchasing, e-commerce, and finding informative content on the Web. Designers used to create a desktop version and then remove heavy-duty elements to create a watered-down version for mobile devices. But with the advent of online marketing and social media, mobile phones and tablets have gained prominence. Studies suggest that most internet traffic comes through mobile phones and tablets—they have largely surpassed desktop websites. Even web design frameworks such as Bootstrap and Foundation use the mobile-first approach, because the target audience has undergone a major shift from desktop users to mobile users.

Until recently, designers created two sites: one optimized for mobiles and the other for desktops. It is essential to focus more on mobile site optimization than the desktop version. However, this can be tricky if the mobile version is a stripped-down version with fewer features and less content than the desktop site. Moreover, this means you have two URLs for the same site with similar content, so you need to use the canonical tag. In addition, a watered-down mobile site results in a pathetic UX.

Enter *responsive web design*: an excellent alternative that uses a single URL for both the mobile and desktop sites. Responsiveness is rated highly by Google. All the features and content of a desktop site are present on the mobile version, meaning there is no compromise on content display; the site is user friendly and ensures an optimal UX. The bounce rate will be lower, because users can get the same information on mobiles as well as desktops. Because there is only one URL, there is no redirect, resulting in faster page-loading times. Because Google highly recommends this approach, responsive web design is here to stay. Currently, Google marks websites as mobile-friendly in mobile searches to help its users identify which websites are likely to work best on their device.

Site-Loading Speed

Site- or page-loading speed is an important attribute, because Google and other search engines penalize sites that take a long time to load. An optimal page-load time leads to better conversion and improves the salability of your products. Pages that take a long time to load may frustrate users and cause negative UX, leading to higher bounce rates. Loss of internet traffic or a bad user experience can damage the site's reputation.

There are several ways you can improve your page-load speed:

- Minifying CSS, JavaScript, and other files

- Minimizing HTTP requests

- Using an efficient server configuration and good bandwidth

- Archiving redundant data in the database, and cleaning out trash and spam

- Using fewer plug-ins and third-party utilities

- Interchanging data and images, depending on the screen size

- Avoiding inline styles, and keeping presentation separate from markup

- Using a content delivery network (CDN)

Off-Page SEO

Whereas on-page SEO and on-site SEO factors are based on the elements and content on your web page or site, off-page SEO factors are external and help you rank higher in SERPs. They are not design or code related and are more like promotional concepts. This section looks at the following (see Figure 3-8):

- Social media

- Blogging

- Localization and local citations

- Inbound links

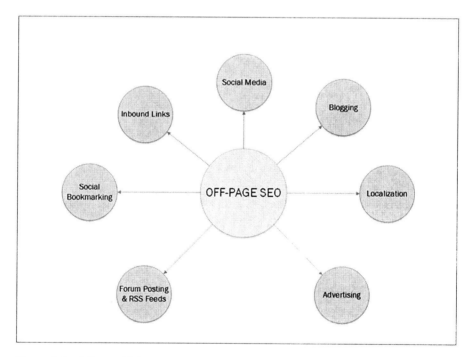

Figure 3-8. *Off-page SEO*

Social Media

Expand your reach by taking advantage of social media optimization and marketing. Social media is an amazing medium with an ever-increasing scope. You can indulge in networking and increase your connections considerably. Reaching out to the modern target audience is beneficial because users can share and promote your website.

Keep your audience engaged, and share updates with them. For example, Facebook and LinkedIn can be awesome utilities that let you expand your business horizons significantly. Share updates and keep your users in the loop using Twitter. You can use the capabilities of these social media sites for branding and advertising for a fraction of the cost of traditional marketing methods such as television advertising, press releases, and Yellow Pages listings. (Chapter 11 discusses social media marketing.)

Blogging

Blogging is an excellent tool for achieving user engagement. You can keep users abreast of the latest trends and technologies in your niche. Informative content on blogs acts as supplementary information about your products or services. Troubleshooting steps, product-relevant content, and meaningful information are some of the elements that can be included on a blog. A plethora of blogging domains and tools can help you reach out to your audience. Inbound and relevant links from your blog to your site can boost your SEO implementation significantly.

Localization and Citations

Local SEO is an important off-page factor because it caters to the user's region. It is a boon especially for small- and medium-size enterprises because it helps them connect with users in their vicinity. Google My Business allows you to list your business and gain prominence in SERPs. You can place your products or services and categorize them so that they show up when a search query is used for that category or niche in the region. Information such as working hours, updates, and contact information can be provided, leading to better accessibility.

Local citations are brand mentions or reviews that educate users about product robustness or attributes. Local SEO utilities such as Yelp and Foursquare are extremely helpful for understanding the pros and cons of your products or services, courtesy of user feedback or input. Reviews help you establish a connection with users and understand their viewpoint and concerns related to your business. Increasing interaction with your users will help streamline your business in the long run.

Inbound Links

Inbound links are links from other domains pointing toward your website. Links from domains with high page rank and authority are preferable and lend more credibility than links from domains with low authority or low page rank. The number of domains that link to your website can be a crucial factor. Studies suggest that links from several different domains to your site can boost your SEO implementation. However, you should not indulge in link farming or use underhanded techniques, which may result in a penalty. There should not be too many links from a single domain, because this is an indication of spamming and can have negative consequences. Referral links from blogs, social media sites, and news aggregators are handy, provided they are relevant and contextual. Inbound links from another domain's home page or key pages are more useful than links from a sidebar or an insignificant page location. Google recommends getting links from domains with high-quality content. Forums, reviews, and comments can contain links pointing to your website and enhance your site presence, provided they are not irrelevant. Backlinks from social bookmarking sites (such as Reddit) and web directories (such as DMOZ) can affect visibility positively.

Summary

This chapter looked at on-page, on-site, and off-page factors that are important for SEO implementation. Case studies hint that more than 250 ranking factors determine the rankings on SERPs. Although the factors remain a business secret, you now have a basic understanding of them and how they help ensure a satisfactory user experience. SEO rules change every year, but the fundamentals remain the same: concentrate on user intent and user experience, because SEO is increasingly tending toward that paradigm.

CHAPTER 4

▓ ▓ ▓

Introducing the Google Tools Suite

There are many search engines, but Google remains the undisputed leader in the worldwide search industry (barring a few, such as Baidu in China and Yandex in Russia). Google is the dominant engine, controlling more than 70% of the search market share. It is "batteries included" and offers a suite of utilities that can boost your SEO processes. This chapter looks at some of the most powerful Google tools that belong in the SEO expert's arsenal:

- Google My Business

- Google AdWords Keyword Planner

- Google Trends

- PageSpeed Insights

- Google Analytics

- Google Search Console

Google My Business

Google My Business is a new portal for local and nonlocal businesses (*local* businesses are those present in the vicinity of the user or in the same geolocation). It is a complete ecosystem for local business or brands. It replaces Google Local and Google Places, other than mainstream integration with Google+ (a social networking site by Google).

Aimed at small- and medium-size enterprises that lack the budget of large-scale organizations, Google My Business helps you reach out to consumers. It is a platform that helps you connect to and interact with customers in addition to promoting your business. You can add pictures of your businesses, post reviews, engage with users, share updates and news, and help your business gain visibility in Google search results.

Figure 4-1 shows the business listings for steel companies in Toronto that resulted from a search query. The boxed listings are prominent, and their location is marked on the map. You also see the operating hours for some businesses and other information such as websites and directions.

© Aravind Shenoy and Anirudh Prabhu 2016
A. Shenoy and A. Prabhu, *Introducing SEO*, DOI 10.1007/978-1-4842-1854-9_4

37

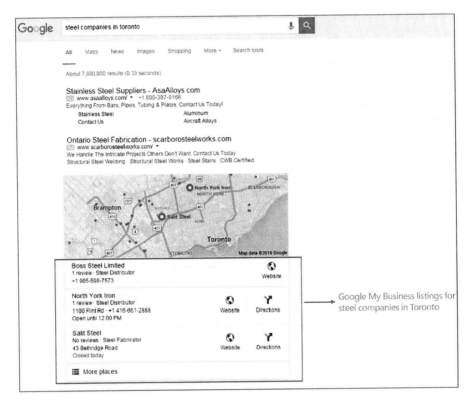

Figure 4-1. *Google My Business listings*

Google My Business is a lucrative platform. To begin using it, the first thing you need to do is verify your business. You can do so via a postcard, with a phone call, or by using instant or bulk verification, if your website is verified by the Google Search Console utility (previously called Google Webmaster Tools).

If you have registered your business in Google Places or Google+, it will automatically be upgraded to Google My Business. You can update your business details as well as indicate the opening and operating hours. You can fill in the business description, post photos of your brand or website, and reach out to customers in several ways. You can offer discounts, offers, deals, and other promotions to expand your user base. You can interact with consumers by responding to their feeds. Integration with Google+ and Google Hangout enables you to keep your customers in sync and address any complaints as well as communicate with them on a regular basis. In addition, Google Apps for Work can be integrated with this platform.

You manage all this using a single interface. Figure 4-2 shows the login page at https://www.google.com/business/.

Figure 4-2. *Google My Business login page*

Google AdWords Keyword Planner

Google AdWords Keyword Planner is a good resource for coming up with keywords for a new project or relevant terms for an existing campaign. You can use this utility to develop terms and filter them for a specific country or region based on the geolocation. You can determine the search volume for keywords and predict the bid for those terms, if you are opting for a paid campaign.

Google AdWords Keyword Planner helps you choose multiple terms that can be used in conjunction with another term, specifically long-tail terms that can drive the right traffic to your website. You can also find alternate terms for your products or services that have low competition and may require less effort to rank well in SERPs. Monthly global and local monthly searches are handy because you can determine the keywords your competitors are using to promote their products and services.

You can find the utility at the following link: `https://adwords.google.com/KeywordPlanner`.

Figure 4-3 shows a snippet of the interface for Google AdWords Keyword Planner.

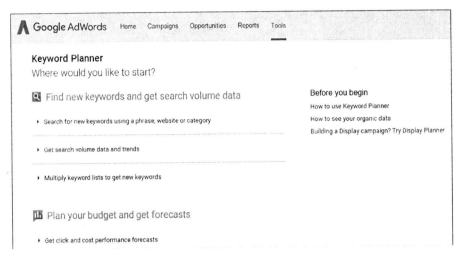

Figure 4-3. *Google AdWords Keyword Planner*

Google Trends

Google Trends is a utility that helps you compare the flow, trends, and popularity of terms and phrases; you can see at a glance how terms and phrases fare. It spans several categories, such as business, nature, sports, travel, and news. You can streamline your keyword research by using Google Trends results along with the Google AdWords Keyword Planner utility. You can even filter search trends by sorting terms geographically or according to time span and categories. For example, you can determine the popularity of terms in a particular country, region, or city.

In addition to finding regional trends, you can use Google Trends for content creation and content development. For example, you can write blogs or include trendy terms in forums and social bookmarking sites. Or you can base content on popular terms or phrases in your new campaigns. You can gain insight into your competitors' trends and compare your business trends with those of your rivals.

You can access Google Trends at `https://www.google.com/trends/`. Figure 4-4 shows a snippet of the home page.

Figure 4-4. *Google Trends home page*

Suppose you want to compare three companies—Facebook, Google, and Microsoft in the United States since 2015 in the News Search category. Figure 4-5 shows the comparison graph.

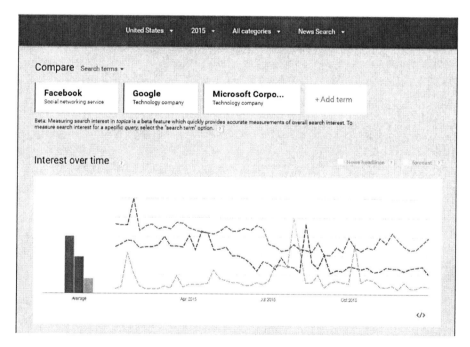

Figure 4-5. *Comparing Facebook, Google, and Microsoft in News Search since 2015*

PageSpeed Insights

Google stresses the importance of web page performance, and its algorithms favor websites with optimal site speed and user experience (UX) design. Optimal Page-loading time counts toward an enhanced UX. Studies suggest that optimal page-load time leads to more conversions, thereby affecting sales significantly. Page speed depends on several factors ranging from web-hosting facility and website design to the hardware used for that site. In particular, websites that take a lot of time to open on mobile devices are penalized, because they result in a bad UX.

Google has its own tool that you can use, not only for site speed but also for other UX factors (see Figure 4-6). You can access the PageSpeed tool at `https://developers.google.com/speed/pagespeed/insights/`.

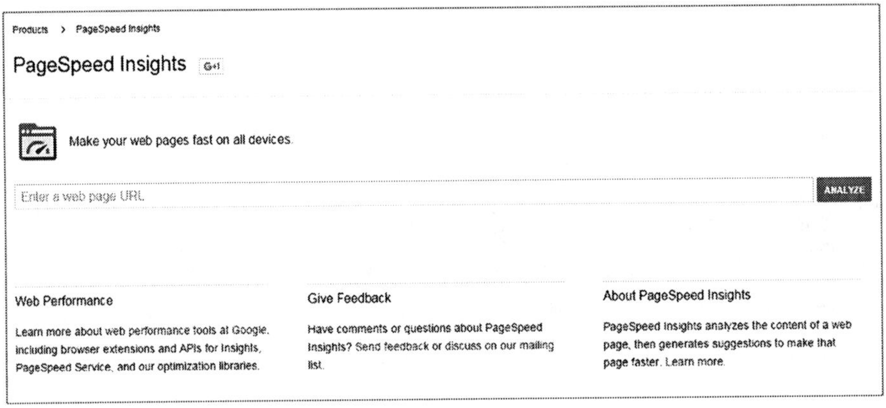

Figure 4-6. *PageSpeed Insights*

Enter a URL or web page address in the search box, and click Analyze. You will see results for mobile and desktop versions. The results include two sections: Speed and User Experience. Fixes as well as suggestions pertaining to speed and UX are listed. Fixes include compression of JavaScript and CSS, avoiding plug-ins for platform compatibility, using legible font sizes, and avoiding landing page redirects. Suggestions are recommendations to further enhance the website for an optimal UX. Figure 4-7 shows a snippet of some example results.

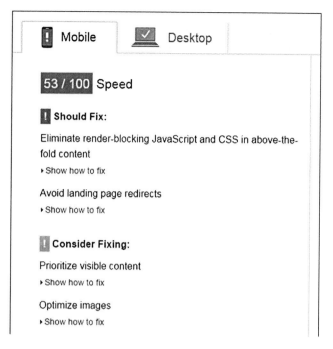

Figure 4-7. *PageSpeed Insights results*

User satisfaction is a prime factor for any business, and it applies to SEO too. Good site speed leads to backlinks, conversion optimization, and favorable reviews, thereby streamlining the UX.

Google Analytics

If you have a website, then you want to know how many people are viewing or buying stuff on that site. You also want to know the geographic location of your users and which content is frequently accessed. Whether your campaigns lead to sales conversions and high traffic can be a deciding factor, especially for an e-commerce site. Enter Google Analytics: an enterprise-grade toolkit that helps you gain insight into your website traffic, history trends, and site statistics. You can find out about pages that have poor traffic and bounce rates and get information about the search query keywords used most often to reach your website. You can learn whether you need a mobile site or, if you already have one, how to optimize it to gain relevant traffic. Traffic trends and links from referral sites can be measured for conversion optimization. You can set custom goals and events to get meaningful information to streamlining your business processes. Tracking metrics and visitor engagement can help you improve your marketing strategy. In short, Google Analytics is a robust utility that helps you make data-driven decisions to enhance your web presence.

This section looks at how to install Google Analytics and incorporate it into your website. First you need a Google account; for example, if you use Gmail, YouTube, Google Drive or any Google primary service, you can use that account for Analytics. However, always make sure you have complete access to and control over that account. The business or website owner should be the only person who fully controls that primary account so that they have access to it at any time from any location.

If you do not have a primary Google account, create one, and make sure you control every aspect of that account. Sign in, and you are directed to the steps shown in Figure 4-8.

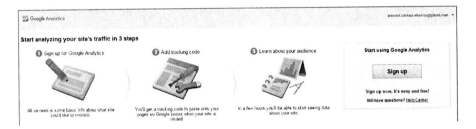

Figure 4-8. *Google Analytics home page*

At right is the Sign Up button. Click it, and you see the page shown in Figure 4-9.

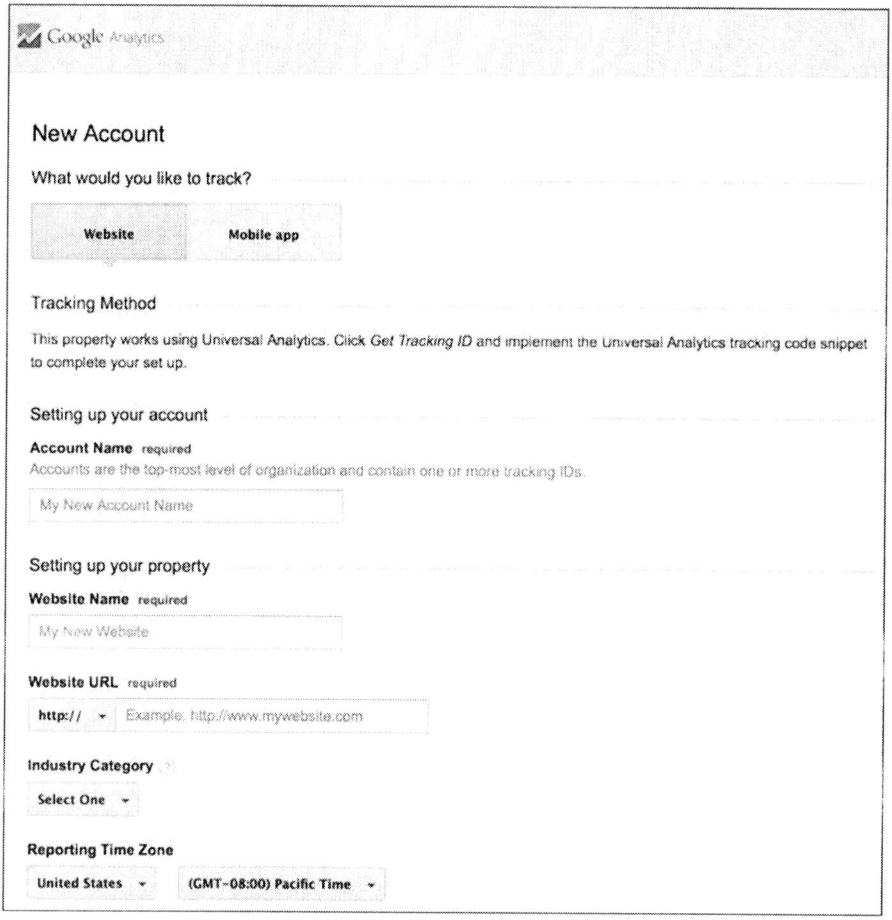

Figure 4-9. *Filling in website information*

In Figure 4-9, you can see two options: Website and Mobile App. Select Website (the default) if you want to set up Analytics for your website. Enter the account name in the Account Name text box, and then entire the name of your website in the Website Name field. Next, enter the web address or URL in the Website URL text box. Select the name of the industry from the Industry Category drop-down menu, and select the Time Zone. Choose the appropriate Data Sharing Settings, and then click the Get Tracking ID button. When you do, you're given a tracking code for verification purposes (see Figure 4-10).

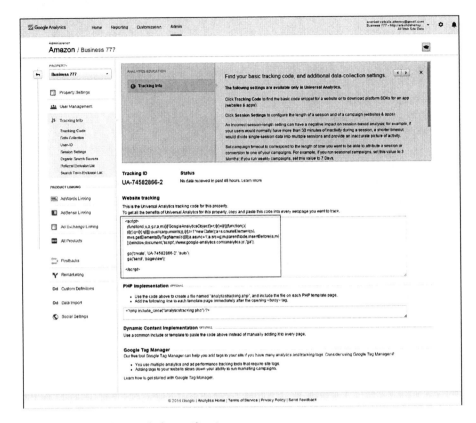

Figure 4-10. *Tracking code for verification*

Once you receive a tracking code, depending on your content management system (CMS), you need to incorporate the tracking code into your document. If you are using Wordpress, you can use the Google Analytics by Yoast plug-in. If you built your site with simple HTML markup, then you need to include the tracking code in the <head> section of your HTML document, just before the closing </head> tag. The following post explains the procedure for installing Google Analytics for different platforms: www.lizlockard. com/installing-google-analytics-on-any-website/.

Next, verify your account using the options in the Google Search Console (discussed in the next section). Once you have set up Google Analytics, you can add users and set permissions. You can define goals to understand when important actions occur on your site.

You can set up Site Search, which helps you gain insight about searches made on your website. You can get an analysis in a day, provided your setup is implemented correctly.

Every time you log in to your account, go to the Reporting section to view the Dashboards, Shortcuts, Audience, Acquisition, Behavior, and Conversion menu items. Figure 4-11 shows the menu for the Reporting section.

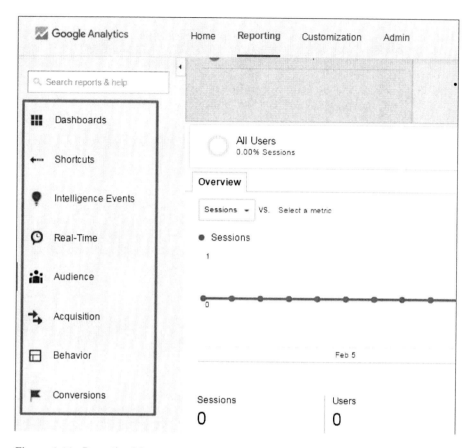

Figure 4-11. *Reporting Menu*

Following are some common terms you will come across while viewing analyzing these reports:

- *Dimensions*: An attribute of your site visitors that can have various values. For example, gender, browser, city, and so on.

- *Metrics*: A measure of elements of a dimension. For example, new users, bounce rate, sessions, and so on.

- *Sessions*: Period of user engagement with the website for a specific date range. For example, time taken for page view during a certain date range.

- *Conversions*: Count of the goals completed on your website. For example, purchasing items on an e-commerce site can be a goal, and conversions relate to users who have visited the site and bought something.

47

- *Bounce rate*: Percentage of single visits where the site visitor leaves the site without any other action. For example, a user may just click the back button if they do not get relevant information when they visit your site's home page for the first time.

- *Audience*: Report items that provide statistics depending on traffic and help you gain insight into a site visitor's behavior on arrival on your site.

- *Acquisition*: Report items that provide information about the source of traffic, actions performed on the site, and whether conversions occur during the sessions.

In addition to the Reporting menu items, you can create custom reports and custom variables to get the most out of the Analytics data. A plethora of third-party utilities and plug-ins are available, such as reporting tools and products that use the platform for Analytics-based tracking. In addition, there is a Google Analytics premium platform that enterprise-grade and large-scale organizations can use to obtain advanced results.

Google Search Console

Google Search Console (formerly known as Google Webmaster Tools [GWT]) is a free utility to analyze your website's indexing and manage and monitor your site's Google Search ranking. It helps you probe and gain insight into how your site appears to the Google search engine. You can also get information related to hack attacks, penalties, and broken links, along with suggestions that can help you improve and manage the presence of your website.

To use Google Search Console, you need to have a primary Google account. Once you log in to the Search Console for the first time, you see the web page shown in Figure 4-12.

Figure 4-12. Search Console Welcome page

Add your website or app by entering the address in the text box (see Figure 4-13).

Figure 4-13. Adding a property

Click Add Property, and then verify that you are the rightful owner or an authority that has complete access to the website. The recommended method is to verify using an HTML file upload (see Figure 4-14). Otherwise, you can click the Alternate Methods tab to can see the other verification methods.

Search Console

Verify your ownership of **http://www.aravindshenoy.wordpress.com/.** Learn more

| Recommended method | Alternate methods |

Recommended: HTML file upload

Upload an HTML file to your site.

1. **Download** this HTML verification file. [google09c58ea1fa812566.html]
2. **Upload** the file to http://www.aravindshenoy.wordpress.com/
3. **Confirm** successful upload by visiting http://www.aravindshenoy.wordpress.com/google09c58ea1fa812566.html in your browser.
4. **Click** Verify below.

To stay verified, don't remove the HTML file, even after verification succeeds.

VERIFY   Not now

Figure 4-14. Recommended methods for verification

The alternate methods to verify the account are as follows (see Figure 4-15):

- HTML tag
- Domain name provider
- Google Analytics
- Google Tag Manager

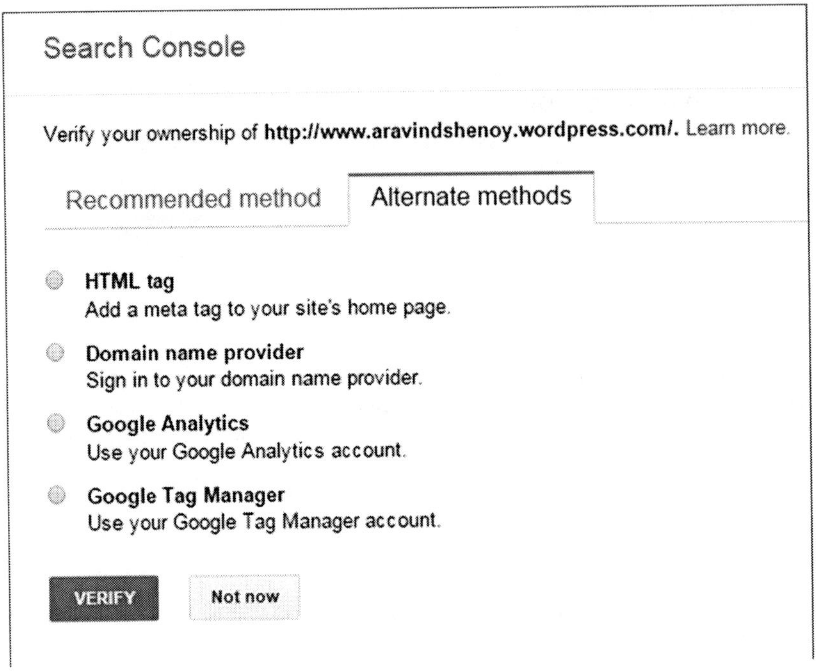

Figure 4-15. *Alternative methods of verification*

Once you verify the account, you can see the Dashboard, which has the features shown in Figure 4-16.

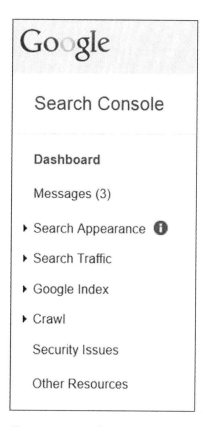

Figure 4-16. *Attributes on the Dashboard*

Let's look at the various features that can help you streamline the SEO process using Google Search Console.

Search Appearance

This section looks at the factors that determine how your site appears to the search engine.

Structured Data

All the structured data for your website is found on this page. The utility helps you gain insight into the structured data elements and defects related to the markup. You can download a report to view errors associated with structured data elements on your site.

Data Highlighter

This feature is useful because it helps you implement structured data if you cannot access the back end.

HTML Improvements

All HTML-related errors, such as title tag errors, lack of opening and closing tags, meta descriptions, and non-indexable content, are flagged. You can then make changes as per the generated report.

Sitelinks

Sitelinks are shortcuts generated by Google and used for deep website navigation. You can even sitelinks to a specific page if you find them irrelevant or incorrect.

Search Traffic

This attribute helps you gauge the keyword search phrases used to make your page visible in search results. You also see a count of how many times your website is reflected in the search results using specific keyword phrases. The Click Through Rate, backlinks, and inbound links from different domains are listed in this section. You can also estimate the number of internal links in your website and learn about basic analytics for your site.

Search Analytics

In this section, you can view organic traffic and filter it according to devices, region, and type of platform (desktop or mobile). You can gain insight into trends and performance of your website in the search results.

Links to Your Site

Here you find information about inbound links and the domains from which these links originate. You can also get information about the anchor text pointing to your website and pages with the highest-valued inbound links.

Manual Actions

This section is crucial because messages related to Google penalizing your website are delivered here. You also see suggestions regarding appropriate fixes related to any penalties.

International Targeting

The hreflang attribute is used to identify the language along with the geographical targeting of each web page. The second tab (Country) is handy if you want to attract a customer base from a specific country. For example, domains that are generic have .com and .org extensions, whereas extensions such as .in, .uk, and .fr (for India, United Kingdom, and France, respectively) are used to target specific countries.

Mobile Usability

You can find out whether your website is mobile friendly. You can see its various drawbacks from the mobile point of view along with an overview of those issues. Mobile data is used more than desktop versions, so Google considers mobile usability a crucial ranking factor.

Google Index

This feature helps you get information about the pages of your site that have already been indexed and also helps you remove URLs that are inappropriate or incorrect.

Index Status

Here you can identify pages that Google has indexed on your site.

Content Keywords

You can gain insight into keywords or phrases often found on your site.

Blocked Resources

Pages on your site that are configured to be blocked by using a robots.txt file (Robots Exclusion Standards) are reflected in this section. For example, tracking programs, external scripts, and private pages are some examples of blocked resources that need not be indexed by Google.

Remove URLs

You can remove pages that are not supposed to be indexed using this feature. For example, if you want to remove a web page that has been indexed, you initially need to block it by configuring it in the robots.txt file. Then you can send a request for removal of that specific URL.

Crawl

Prior to the indexing of your web pages, the pages need to be scanned or crawled by Google bots or spiders. Information related to the crawling of your site can be viewed here.

Crawl Errors

This attribute indicates any errors that were found while crawling your web pages: for example, a "404 Page not found" error. Once you fix the errors, you can update Google.

Crawl Stats

This indicates the number of pages crawled for a certain period. It also indicates the download time and the size of the download.

Fetch As Google

This attribute is handy for understanding how Google renders a web page. Instead of Fetch, you can use Fetch and Render to enable Google to crawl and display the web pages, akin to a browser rendering the pages.

You can see the difference between rendering the page with Google and with a browser, helping you boost the SEO processes for your site.

Robots.txt Tester

This attribute checks for defects in your `robots.txt` file.

Sitemaps

This facility helps you submit the XML sitemap of your site to Google. It makes it easy for Google bots to dig deep, because it makes web pages more accessible to those bots. Errors related to the submitted sitemap are also reflected in this section.

URL Parameters

Although Google bots can usually understand URL parameters, if there is any ambiguity, you can explicitly configure parameters using this section so that the Google search engine understands them more efficiently. For example, suppose a user is on an e-commerce portal and wants to shop for athletic shoes. The user can use filters such as the sole material, leather or synthetic, color, and price of those shoes. The filters when used lead to represent a different URL to the user; however, strings appended to the URL due to using combinations of filters show different URLs to users for the same or duplicate content. Google has a workaround for this. Similar URLs are grouped in a cluster, and then Google decides the best URL in that cluster to represent the cluster group. In case of ambiguity, if Google is unable to decide the best URL for that cluster, you can use the URL Parameters facility to specify which URL should be used to represent a group.

Security Issues

If your site is hacked or there is some other issue like a malware attack, you can find information and the suggestions for fixing it in this section.

Site Settings

In the upper-right section of the page is a gear icon that leads to Site Settings. You can choose between www and non-www versions of your website. This is done so that both sites are treated the same. For example, if your site's web address is `http://example1234567865.com` and the other link is `http://www.example1234567865.com`, selecting one as the preferred domain ensures that both URLs are treated the same. However, you need to verify that you are the rightful owner and authority for both sites. You can also set the crawl rate here, so Google will crawl pages keeping in sync with the bandwidth of your site.

Google Search Console is a vast topic by itself and is a vital tool for understanding the nuances of your website.

Summary

This chapter looked at the significant set of Google tools available for your use. You learned about the Google My Business feature before moving to the Keyword Planner. Then you saw the Google Trends toolkit and learned about PageSpeed Insights. Finally, you looked at the most important tools: Google Search Console and Google Analytics. In the next chapter, you learn about obstacles you may encounter when using SEO.

CHAPTER 5

Obstacles in SEO

There are certain blips you come across when implementing SEO in projects. These hurdles hinder the SEO workflow significantly and can affect your website's visibility. SEO associates tend to tweak websites for search engines and forget to focus on the user experience. An appropriate approach is to design the website for users (user-centric) and then tweak the website for search engines.

There are several botlenecks that we tend to overlook when we are implementing SEO. These bottlenecks can be game-changers that reduce your site's visibility in SERPs. In this chapter, we will discuss the obstacles in SEO and include suggestions to overcome these drawbacks.

Black-Hat SEO

Despite knowing that black-hat SEO will result in penalties, some SEO experts resort to underhanded techniques. Link farming, cloaking, keyword stuffing, irrelevant content, and spamming are black-hat techniques that are still in use. The results may seem positive, but eventually Google and other search engines realize that they are being duped, resulting in a penalty.

Let's consider the *cloaking* black-hat SEO technique. It is akin to *spamdexing*, where the content presented to search engine crawlers is different than the content presented to human users. It is a deceitful way of achieving higher rankings: the content delivered is different depending on IP addresses or HTTP headers. This manipulative technique tries to trick search engines into believing that the content is the same as what users see.

Another black-hat SEO technique is *link farming*, where sites exchange reciprocal links to boost their rankings by fooling the search engines. It is different from *link building*, which is an organic way of boosting rankings. Because search engines such as Google and Bing rank sites based on their popularity and inbound links, some SEO consultants used to implement link farming to get links from hundreds of websites that were not even slightly related to the target site. Some SEO consultants also had link farms that used devious ways of exchanging links with other sites, something like a link-exchange program.

For example, suppose a site is devoted to troubleshooting Windows OS issues. If inbound links come from sites such as Stack Overflow, authority sites, and relevant blogs, then they are legitimate. However, if such a site receives inbound links from travel and tourism sites offering vacation packages in Miami or from sites offering plumbing solutions in Ibiza, then there is no relevance—the sites have no connection. Therefore,

© Aravind Shenoy and Anirudh Prabhu 2016
A. Shenoy and A. Prabhu, *Introducing SEO*, DOI 10.1007/978-1-4842-1854-9_5

such sites use link farming and are deceitful because they just want to boost their rankings using these underhanded techniques.

Instead of fooling the search engines, it is better to use white-hat SEO techniques that are beneficial in the long run. Quality link building, using social media appropriately, and engaging users with solid content are some of the white-hat SEO techniques. It may take weeks or even months for the results to show, but white-hat techniques are the norms that SEO experts must follow to gain visibility in SERPs.

Irrelevant Content

Content is king. However, if you use duplicate content or inappropriate methods such as keyword stuffing in your content, you are bound to be penalized. Content must be relevant and must engage users. Fresh content is also an essential factor, because the search engines show an affinity for fresh, quality content. Write content for users, and then tweak it to optimize it for the search engines.

Targeting the Wrong Audience

Your SEO implementation must be optimized for an appropriate target audience. If you do not target the right audience, your efforts will be wasted. For example, gaming consoles, portable music players, and MP3 gadgets are appealing to youth, whereas long-term retirement plans are better suited for middle-aged users.

Competition

Small- and medium-sized businesses do not have a huge budget for advertising their products and services. Therefore, they need to ensure that they do not try the same approaches as large-scale enterprises that have a panel of SEO experts, funding, and expensive advertising methods. You should also avoid using metadata and content similar to that of large-scale enterprises, because doing so will hinder your SEO process.

Using keywords prevalent in the web pages of enterprise-grade organizations is detrimental because small enterprises do not have the budget, web presence, and reach for mass-scale advertising to outperform large adversaries. You can use Google My Business and other Google tools (as well as third-party enhancements) to gain visibility. You can also use keywords that have less competition and target a niche market. You may see your website gain prominence on SERPs using such low-competition keywords.

Overlooking Social Media as a Medium

Social media marketing is no longer an optional method. It is mandatory to take advantage of the scope and reach of social media to create awareness of your brand. Many organizations neglect social media, and this limits exposure to your site. This doesn't mean you should over-optimize social media strategies by using every social media app in the market. You also have to be relevant.

For example, you can advertise by using a concise video about your product or service on YouTube. You can tweet about your latest product update on Twitter or write a blog on WordPress that is relevant to your product. Users love to read fresh and engaging content, and so do the search engines. You can also use backlinks to your site and outbound links to relevant sites (such as linking a term to Wikipedia), which will benefit users looking for informative content.

Ignoring UX for Your Website

Your site may have lots of jazzy features, but if your users cannot navigate easily or find it difficult to access content, then the result may be a shabby UX. For example, the Add To Cart button on an e-commerce website must be easily accessible to users. UX is a crucial factor for search engines because they like sites that are popular and have a high degree of usability.

Missing XML and HTML Sitemaps

XML and HTML sitemaps are designed for search engines and users, respectively. Your site may have the latest updates and game-changing features, but if the search engines are unable to crawl and map your site, that is detrimental to your SEO workflow. You must submit XML and HTML sitemaps to the search engines, so your deep web pages can be crawled more easily. (Chapter 6 is dedicated to sitemaps.)

Slow Page-Load Time

Slow page-load time is a deterrent to SEO processes. Code-heavy pages, uncompressed and unoptimized HTML, images, external embedded media, extensive use of Flash, and JavaScript result in slow page-loading times. There can be other factors, too, that may result in high page-load times: using server-centric dynamic scripts, non-optimal web hosting, and lack of required bandwidth. These factors negatively affect your SEO processes and are major hindrances resulting in lower rankings. For example, SEO experts recommend 2 to 3 seconds as the optimal loading time for product pages on e-commerce sites after analyzing statistics from research and analytics.

Moreover, surveys and studies related to site speed infer that users tend to abandon a site that isn't loaded within 3 to 4 seconds. This also represents a shabby user experience, resulting in lower conversions and sales.

Using Flash on Your Site

In the early days of the web, Flash was an awesome resource that helped site build intuitive modules and impressive page elements. However, with the advent of HTML5, this cutting-edge utility has taken a backseat. Moreover, as the mobile and tablet market has become a dominant force, the use of Flash is considered redundant, because Flash was tailored for desktop users.

Flash is more prone to malicious malware hacking, from a security point of view. Its non-scalable features mean you cannot minimize or expand it or set a viewport for it. Everything you can do in Flash can be done more quickly and easily in HTML5. You can also use the latest web design frameworks to build interactive sites, thereby relegating Flash to the sidelines. Google and other search engines cannot read Flash, although recently, Google claims it can index the text in Flash files. Considering the pitfalls associated with Flash, you should use HTML5 to design and develop interactive sites with enhanced animation and special effects.

JavaScript Accessibility Issues

Client-side JavaScript, extensively used in single-page applications, helps you build dynamic and highly intuitive websites. However, search engines cannot parse JavaScript-generated content efficiently. Currently, only Google's search engine is able to understand JavaScript, albeit at a more basic level. With frameworks such as Angular and Ember being used to build dynamic web pages, search engines will have to develop the ability to understand complex JavaScript; so far, this ability is evolving. There are a few workarounds you can implement to tackle JavaScript accessibility issues.

Suppose your browser is an old version and cannot parse the latest features and functions of JavaScript. You can use fallback code (also called *polyfills*) to replicate the content of JavaScript-based web applications. Using fallback code is an option for tackling the JavaScript issue using server-side rendering. However, it requires a lot of effort and costs more because you must develop code for all the features on the website; plus there is heavy code maintenance. It also makes your pages code-heavy, resulting in higher page-loading times.

Another aspect to be considered is the workaround for applications built using JavaScript frameworks such as Angular and Backbone. When search engines and social networks crawl your pages, they only see the JavaScript tags. To ensure that these dynamic pages are accessible to the search engines, you can use a prerendering service such as Prerender (https://prerender.io/) or SEO.js (http://getseojs.com/).

The Prerender middleware checks all requests and, if there is a request from a search engine spider or bot, sends a request to Prerender.io for the static HTML for that JavaScript page. The Prerender service uses PhantomJS to create static HTML, which in turn is submitted to the spiders for crawling. Prerender can be used for most of the JavaScript frameworks.

An alternative to Prerender is SEO.js. Once you submit a website to the SEO. js dashboard, the utility service visits your web pages and creates HTML screenshots for each page. An added advantage is that the snapshots are updated automatically. Therefore, when a search engine's spiders or bots visit your site, they see only fully rendered content from the snapshot. You can also use SEO.js to create XML sitemaps to enhance the accessibility of your web pages to the spiders.

Now that you have learned the core obstacles that hinder SEO, let's look at Google's Accelerated Mobile Pages (AMP): a new concept that will change the face of the mobile web.

AMP

Accelerated Mobile Pages (AMP) is a Google project aimed at the mobile web. Akin to the concept of Facebook's Instant Articles and Apple's Apple News, AMP pages will change the way people perceive the mobile web. AMP pages are web-based, meaning they are rendered in a browser. They are independent documents that are sourced from your web server. Optionally, you can store AMP documents in a CDN cache to render them more quickly.

AMP pages are made up of the following modules:

- AMP HTML

- AMP Runtime

- AMP Cache

While responsive websites face issues such as rendering heavy-duty desktop content on a mobile website, JavaScript bloat, and sluggish speed on the mobile platform, AMP pages are designed for the mobile platform and help users view site pages efficiently across various mobile and tablet sizes. JavaScript is baked-in for AMP Runtime, which manages the loading of AMP modules along with features such as runtime validation for AMP HTML. It defines the priority for resource loading, thereby resulting in an optimal page-loading experience. AMP HTML documents can be stored on your server, and you can use your own CDN; but you can also take advantage of the benefits of using Google's CDN, which streamlines the SEO processes built around these pages. When you search a page on Google, you see the results on desktop browsers. However, on the mobile platform, there is a high probability that Google will direct you to AMP pages rather than regular pages, because AMP load instantaneously and the Runtime streamlines the utilization of available resources.

Unlike Facebook's Instant Articles or Apple's Apple News, AMP pages (although backed by Google) are portal-agnostic and open-source. They are supposed to be built-in with ads and analytics support. AMP are accessible from any portal: Google Search, Pinterest, or anywhere online. In summary, AMP pages are a lucrative alternative to heavy-duty websites; they display information quickly and render content effectively without the bulk or clutter.

Go to www.theedesign.com/blog/2016/year-of-google-amp to see the difference between a normal web page and an AMP page. You can find out more at https://www.ampproject.org/

Summary

This chapter looked at several factors that create obstacles to SEO success. However, they are not set in stone. More obstacles will arise as time goes by, because SEO is an ongoing process. You also looked at the concept of AMP pages, which are a diet version of a website tailored for the mobile platform. The next chapter looks at HTML and XML sitemaps and how they help the SEO process.

CHAPTER 6

Sitemaps

A *sitemap* contains a list of pages within a website. A sitemap can exist in a form accessible to crawlers, humans, or both. Typically, a sitemap is hierarchical in nature.

The purpose of a sitemap is to display, how the website is organized apart from navigation and labeling. It provides clarity about the relationship between various website pages and components. Certain types of sitemaps, such as XML sitemaps, provide additional information about the pages in a website, such as the last update and frequency of updating.

Sitemaps tell search engines about the content type on the listed pages: for example, audio, video, or image. The information displayed about an image or a video content type may include the video duration, category, age rating, image description, type, and licensing details.

Search engines crawlers (also known as bots or spiders) scan and discover most web pages. However, broken links can stall the discovery of some pages. A website may contain a lot of pages, a large amount of isolated archived content, or recently launched pages that need to be crawled, or there may be external links that point to it. Also, a website may have rich intuitive content such as media files that need to be crawled. If search engines are not deep-crawling a website, those pages do not populate at the top of the SERPs.

There is no guarantee that all the items in a sitemap will receive enhanced exposure or be crawled, but providing sitemaps is a good practice because it definitely makes it easier for the search engines.

Types of Sitemap

There are two types of sitemaps:

- XML sitemap
- HTML sitemap

An XML sitemap is in an XML format that is tailored for the search engines. It is used to indicate information about various pages. However, it is not user-friendly, because it caters to search engines and not human users. An XML sitemap sheds light on information such as the relationships between pages, their update history, and the frequency with which they are updated.

© Aravind Shenoy and Anirudh Prabhu 2016
A. Shenoy and A. Prabhu, *Introducing SEO*, DOI 10.1007/978-1-4842-1854-9_6

On the other hand, an HTML sitemap is user-friendly and tailored for human users. It helps them find the page containing content they are looking for. Because it is user-friendly, it also makes the website more accessible to spiders.

You need to remember that XML sitemaps cater to search engine crawlers, whereas HTML sitemaps cater to human users. In addition, HTML sitemaps are not supported in the Google Search Console utility.

Difference between HTML and XML Sitemaps

As mentioned earlier, XML sitemaps are developed for search engine spiders and contain the website's page URLs along with additional information such as update history. Listing 6-1 shows the XML sitemap created for one of our client websites, `http://techvictus.com/`.

Listing 6-1. Example XML Sitemap

```
<?xml version="1.0" encoding="UTF-8" ?>
<urlset xmlns="http://www.sitemaps.org/schemas/sitemap/0.9"
xmlns:xsi="http://www.w3.org/2001/XMLSchema-instance"
xsi:schemaLocation="http://www.sitemaps.org/schemas/sitemap/0.9
http://www.sitemaps.org/schemas/sitemap/0.9/sitemap.xsd">
  <url>
    <loc>http://www.techvictus.com/</loc>
    <lastmod>2016-03-12</lastmod>
    <changefreq>daily</changefreq>
    <priority>0.5</priority>
  </url>
  <url>
    <loc>http://www.techvictus.com/about.html</loc>
    <lastmod>2016-03-12</lastmod>
    <changefreq>daily</changefreq>
    <priority>0.5</priority>
  </url>
  <url>
    <loc>http://www.techvictus.com/solution.html</loc>
    <lastmod>2016-03-12</lastmod>
    <changefreq>daily</changefreq>
    <priority>0.5</priority>
  </url>
  <url>
    <loc>http://www.techvictus.com/sns.html</loc>
    <lastmod>2016-03-12</lastmod>
    <changefreq>daily</changefreq>
    <priority>0.5</priority>
  </url>
```

```
  <url>
    <loc>http://www.techvictus.com/partners.html</loc>
    <lastmod>2016-03-12</lastmod>
    <changefreq>daily</changefreq>
    <priority>0.5</priority>
  </url>
  <url>
    <loc>http://www.techvictus.com/training.html</loc>
    <lastmod>2016-03-12</lastmod>
    <changefreq>daily</changefreq>
    <priority>0.5</priority>
  </url>
  <url>
    <loc>http://www.techvictus.com/resource.html</loc>
    <lastmod>2016-03-12</lastmod>
    <changefreq>daily</changefreq>
    <priority>0.5</priority>
  </url>
  <url>
    <loc>http://www.techvictus.com/login.html</loc>
    <lastmod>2016-03-12</lastmod>
    <changefreq>daily</changefreq>
    <priority>0.5</priority>
  </url>
</urlset>
```

An HTML sitemap provides an indexed list of the website's content in addition to the site's navigation. Such a list increases the accessibility of the website from both the user and search engine perspective. For example, it helps users who are browsing a website by providing the list of web pages, which may save time for a user who is looking for a specific page.

Listing 6-2 shows the HTML sitemap for the same website used in the previous listing.

Listing 6-2. Example HTML Sitemap

```
<!DOCTYPE html>
<html xmlns="http://www.w3.org/1999/xhtml">
<head>
<title>Sitemap</title>
</head>
<body>
<a href="http://www.techvictus.com/">Techvictus</a>
<ul>
<li><a href="http://www.techvictus.com/about.html">Techvictus</a></li>
<li><a href="http://www.techvictus.com/solution.html">Techvictus</a></li>
<li><a href="http://www.techvictus.com/sns.html">Techvictus</a></li>
<li><a href="http://www.techvictus.com/partners.html">Techvictus</a></li>
<li><a href="http://www.techvictus.com/training.html">Techvictus</a></li>
```

```
<li><a href="http://www.techvictus.com/resource.html">Techvictus</a></li>
<li><a href="http://www.techvictus.com/login.html">Techvictus</a></li>
</ul>
</body>
</html>
```

Making the Choice

It is a good practice to use both XML and HTML sitemaps for your website. XML sitemaps provide the search engines with information related to all the pages on a website. They also include pages that are not directly connected to the home page, such as posts.

HTML sitemaps, on the other hand, contain a list of pages along with their links. This enables users to visit specific pages on your website, eliminating the hassle of navigating through all the pages. In addition, such a list helps track which pages are being visited the most by users.

Creating a Sitemap

After reading the previous sections, you may be ready to add a sitemap to your website. In this section, you create an HTML sitemap for the http://www.techvictus.com/ website. Listing 6-3 shows the HTML sitemap markup for the website.

Listing 6-3. Creating an HTML Sitemap

```
<!DOCTYPE html>
<html>
<head>
<title>Sitemap</title>
</head>
<body>
<a href="http://www.techvictus.com/">Techvictus</a>
<ul>
<li><a href="http://www.techvictus.com/about.html">Techvictus:About us</a></li>
<li><a href="http://www.techvictus.com/solution.html">Techvictus:Solutions
</a></li>
<li><a href="http://www.techvictus.com/sns.html">Techvictus:Service and
Solutions</a></li>
<li><a href="http://www.techvictus.com/partners.html">Techvictus:Partners
</a></li>
<li><a href="http://www.techvictus.com/training.html">Techvictus:Training
</a></li>
<li><a href="http://www.techvictus.com/resource.html">Techvictus:Resource
</a></li>
<li><a href="http://www.techvictus.com/login.html">Techvictus:Login</a></li>
</ul>
</body>
</html>
```

This HTML sitemap enables users to find the correct path to the content they are looking for. If you want information related to the organization, you can click the About Us link listed in the sitemap.

This sitemap uses the
 (break) tag. Instead of <br>, you can also use the unordered list tag (<ul>); it depends on your preference.

A plethora of sitemap generator tools are available for free on the web. For the previously mentioned site, we used the tool found at http://www.sitemapdoc.com/ (see Figure 6-1).

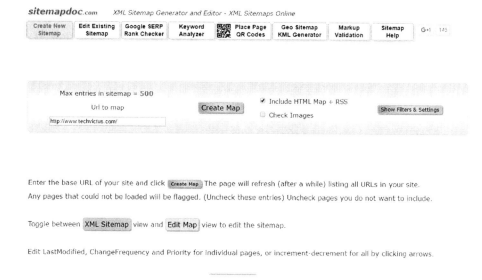

Figure 6-1. *Online tool interface at* sitemapdoc.com

Enter the website URL for which you want the sitemap, with additional filters such as checking images and exclusions. Once you enter all the relevant information, click the Create Map button. Figure 6-2 shows the output.

Figure 6-2. *Output of the sitemap generator*

You have the option to extract XML, HTML, or text versions of the sitemaps by clicking the respective buttons on the page list. If you click the XML Sitemap button, you see the result shown in Figure 6-3.

Figure 6-3. Generated XML sitemap

Once the sitemap is generated, it can be edited, copied, and uploaded to your website server. By default, you need to upload this XML to the root of your website. If you want to upload it elsewhere, you need to add an entry in the `robots.txt` file so the search engine can reach this information. If you generate an HTML sitemap, you can link it to the footer of your web page so users can easily navigate to a particular web page.

Popular Sitemap Generators

Generating a sitemap for a small website is usually not time consuming. However, this can be a very time-consuming activity for large, complex websites. Performing manual sitemap generation on such websites is not only expensive with respect to time, but also prone to errors. In such situations, sitemap generators come in handy. A *sitemap generator* is a tool that takes the URL of the website as input. It then scans the website and lists all the pages it contains in XML or HTML format. This section looks at some of the widely used sitemap generators.

MindNode (`https://mindnode.com/`)

MindNode is a visual tool tailored for Apple devices only (see Figure 6-4). You can build sitemaps as well as plan your projects in a visual appealing way using this utility. The only constraint is that you export to XML. However, you can use the PDF, image, or simple text version generated using this app.

Figure 6-4. MindNode

WriteMaps (`https://writemaps.com/`)

WriteMaps is an efficient utility for online sitemap generation (see Figure 6-5). You can create three sitemaps for free using a single account. Its intuitive character helps you create sitemaps as well as customize colors, map page content, and easily format content. The generated sitemaps can be exported in PDF as well as XML formats.

Figure 6-5. *WriteMaps*

DynoMapper (`https://dynomapper.com/`)

Dyno Mapper is an awesome ecosystem used for creating sitemaps (see Figure 6-6). In addition to building sitemaps, it provides features such as Google Analytics support, website accessibility testing, and keyword tracking that help boost your SEO projects significantly. It comes with drag-and-drop functionality, it can detect broken links, and it provides cloud support with regular content audit input.

Figure 6-6. *Dyno Mapper*

Summary

This chapter gave you a general overview of sitemaps, the different kinds of sitemaps, and some online tools that can assist you in creating interactive, intuitive sitemaps. The next chapter looks at keyword strategies and several factors that are imperative for SEO success.

71

CHAPTER 7

▩ ▩ ▩

Keyword Research and Strategy

Keyword strategy and research rank among the top factors that influence your SEO strategies. Keywords indicate the line of business your website caters to. They help you gain traffic from users looking to buy something or searching informative content on your site.

In Chapter 4, we looked at the Google AdWords Keyword Planner utility. However, Google Keyword Planner often displays terms and phrases related to *seed keywords* (base keywords that form the foundation of terms on your site related to your niche market); these are geared more toward advertising and result in bringing more traffic to the website using non-organic means (pay-per-click or AdWords). For example, if you enter the term **tennis** in Google's Keyword Planner, it displays words that are strongly tied to the keyword. But because almost everyone is using Google Keyword Planner, the results are ambiguous and span a massive range. For example, type in **tennis**, select the United States as the location, and choose the date range January 2015 to January 2016. Click *Get Ideas* to see lists of terms on the Ad Group Ideas and Keyword Ideas tabs, as shown in Figure 7-1.

Ad group ideas	Keyword ideas				Columns ▾	☒	⬇ Download	Add all (726)

Search Terms		Avg. monthly searches Jan 2015 - Jan 2016	Competition		Suggested bid	Ad impr. share	Add to plan
tennis	☒	165,000	Low		52.96	–	»

Show rows 30 ▾   1 - 1 of 1 keywords |< < > >|

Keyword (by relevance)		Avg. monthly searches Jan 2015 - Jan 2016	Competition		Suggested bid	Ad impr. share	Add to plan
tennis live	☒	3,600	Low		12.25	–	»
tennis results	☒	9,900	Low		15.64	–	»
tennis shop	☒	1,300	Medium		72.85	–	»
wimbledon tennis	☒	2,900	Low		45.31	–	»
tennis racquet	☒	22,200	High		65.70	–	»

Figure 7-1. *Keyword Ideas list*

© Aravind Shenoy and Anirudh Prabhu 2016
A. Shenoy and A. Prabhu, *Introducing SEO*, DOI 10.1007/978-1-4842-1854-9_7

The range of keyword ideas is massive, ranging from *Wimbledon*, *Tennis shop*, and *tennis scores* to *tennis news*. Therefore, to use the Keyword Planner efficiently, you need to understand your niche market. Suppose you have a tennis equipment business: then you need to enter a term that targets users interested in tennis equipment. Enter **tennis equipment** instead of **tennis** in the search bar, and you see the keywords shown in Figure 7-2.

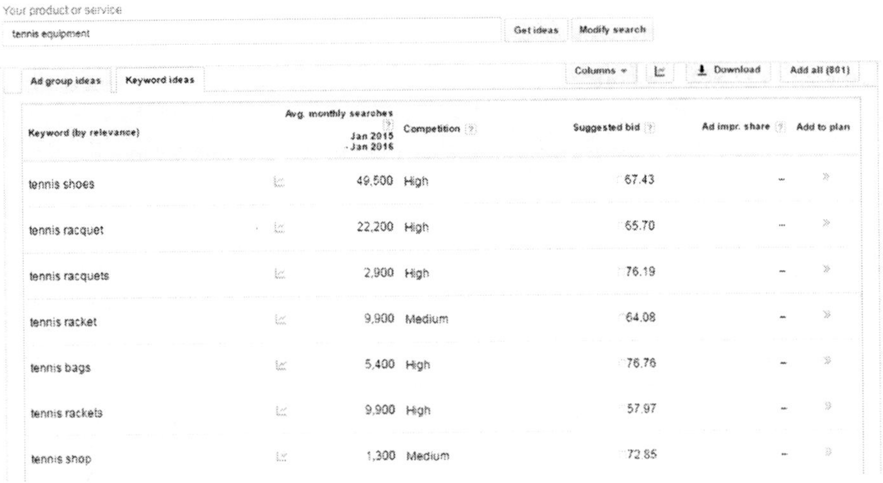

Keyword (by relevance)		Avg. monthly searches [?] Jan 2015 - Jan 2016	Competition [?]	Suggested bid [?]	Ad impr. share [?]	Add to plan
tennis shoes	⌁	49,500	High	67.43	--	»
tennis racquet	⌁	22,200	High	65.70	--	»
tennis racquets	⌁	2,900	High	76.19	--	»
tennis racket	⌁	9,900	Medium	64.08	--	»
tennis bags	⌁	5,400	High	76.76	--	»
tennis rackets	⌁	9,900	High	57.97	--	»
tennis shop	⌁	1,300	Medium	72.85	--	»

Figure 7-2. *Targeting your niche market*

The keywords related to tennis equipment include *tennis shoes, tennis racquet, tennis bags*, and so on. These ideas can help you plan your SEO strategy. (Google Keyword Planner is an awesome utility, and you can achieve much more when you take full advantage of it, but that is outside the scope of this book.) At the same time, you need to understand that results such as *tennis shoes, tennis racquet*, and *tennis bags* are super-competitive. If you are a small company, you cannot match the advertising and reach of enterprise-grade setups. So, targeting these keywords may not give you the desired results. Your keyword strategy is important, and you need to ensure that your website makes the best use of the various keyword-research methods available.

Types of Keywords

Usually, keywords are divided into the following categories: *head*, *body*, and *long-tail* terms.

Head

Head keywords are usually one- or two-word terms that span a massive, generic range. These head keywords are not specific and cater to nothing in particular. For example, the word *tennis* is an example of a head keyword. When you talk about tennis, topics can span such things as Wimbledon, tennis equipment, tennis shops, tennis live broadcasts, and tennis world rankings. Head keywords are used in various topics and are super-competitive but are not good for optimizing conversions.

Body

Body keywords are specific and are limited to two or three words. For example, *online shoe shopping* is a body keyword. Other examples are *black canvas sneakers* and *Shirts online UK*. As you can see, they cater to a specific audience and are apt to be used in SEO projects.

Long Tail

Long-tail keywords are very specific and usually consist of four, five, or more words—for example, *online shoes Aldo Amazon Canada*. These terms are highly specific and are used as search queries by users. Other examples are *Organic Tea India online order Alibaba* and *Reebok black sneakers under $150 Amazon*.

Of these categories, you should target body keywords, because they are not too specific and help you gain a wider audience from various streams. For example, if a user searches for tennis shoes in Toronto, then *Tennis shoes Toronto* may be an example of a body keyword. A long-tail keyword would be something like *Tennis shoes Reebok store Downtown Toronto sale*. See the difference? The body keyword used here is not too localized and can fetch you customers from a target audience all over Toronto, whereas the long-tail keyword is extremely specific and is limited to the Reebok Store in downtown Toronto. Therefore, body keywords are your best bet and may be more useful because they span a sizeable audience.

Sources of Keywords

Finding appropriate keywords can be quite a juggle due to factors such as competition, budget, and search volume. You can look at several avenues to find appropriate keywords. For example, type **tennis equipment** in Google search: in addition to the list of results, at the bottom of the page are other searches related to your search query (see Figure 7-3).

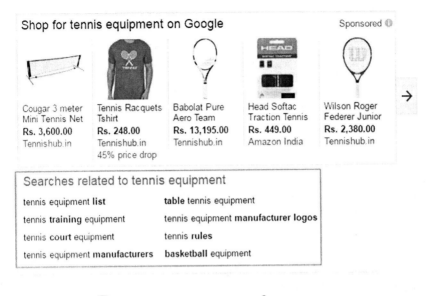

Figure 7-3. *Searches related to the search query*

Thus, you can get information about keywords from various sources. Another way to search is using social bookmarking sites and online Forums. Figure 7-4 shows content on tennis equipment.

Figure 7-4. *Tennis equipment forums*

Figure 7-4 highlights a post on stringing techniques and stringing machines. Such content would be useful for an informative blog on your website. This shows how deep you can delve to get relevant information and keywords for your SEO processes.

Wikipedia, Ezine, eHow, How Stuff Works, Yahoo Answers, Quora, and Stack Exchange are several reliable sources where you can not only find appropriate keywords or long-tail terms but also link anchor text with these sites, thereby giving your site more credibility from an SEO perspective. For example, enter **tennis shoes ezine** in the Google search box. When you check the results, you can find some handy information: Figure 7-5 shows that you can gain some relevant terms that are less competitive but useful for SEO.

How To Chose The Best Pair of Sneakers | Ezine Article Board
www.**ezinearticleboard**.com/.../how-to-chose-the-best-pair-of-**sneakers**/ ▾
Anyone who runs or plays sports will want to use a great couple of **running shoes**. What's more, there are many who may have never jogged each day within ...

Choosing Tennis Shoes - Ezine Articles
ezinearticles.com › Recreation and Sports › Tennis ▾
Oct 13, 2005 - Good **tennis shoes** do several things apart from covering your feet, and tennis is a sport, that is very hard on shoes, and feet, so you need to find ...

Some Interesting Facts About Sneakers! - EzineArticles.com
ezinearticles.com › Shopping and Product Reviews › Fashion Style ▾
Sep 6, 2012 - Walking shoes are completely different from other **athletic sneakers**. Cross trainers and other style of sneakers have a lot of differences in their ...

Learn All You Can About Shoes Here | Ezine.Club
ezine.club/2015/12/01/learn-all-you-can-about-**shoes**-here/
Dec 1, 2015 - **Ezine.Club**. Post and Share Your Articles! Last Updated: December 1, 2015 ... If you wear a lot of **tennis shoes**, buy them from an athletic goods ...

Figure 7-5. *Finding useful keywords and phrases from established sites such as Ezine*

In the highlighted portion of Figure 7-5, you see two terms: *athletic sneakers* and *cross trainers*. These words may have significantly lower search volume compared to *tennis shoes* but can be useful because they have less competition and more relevance.

In addition to Google's Keyword Planner, there are several other tools such as WordStream's suite of keyword tools (Free Keyword Tool, Free Keyword Niche Finder, Free Keyword Grouper, and Negative Keyword Tool), UberSuggest, and Soovle.

Another useful utility is the Keyword Tool at http://keywordtool.io/. Using it, you can generate 750+ body and long-tail terms for each seed keyword for free. Based on the Google platform, this open source tool uses the best of Google AutoComplete and Google Suggest. It also supports multiple languages and multiple search engine portals such as Google, YouTube, Bing, Amazon, and App Store.

Let's look at an example of using this tool to generate niche keywords. Suppose you want to find tennis equipment and shoe stores in the United Kingdom. Enter **tennis shoe stores** as the seed keyword in the text box and select United Kingdom as the location and English as the language. When you generate the keywords for this seed keyword, the result is 89 keywords (see Figure 7-6).

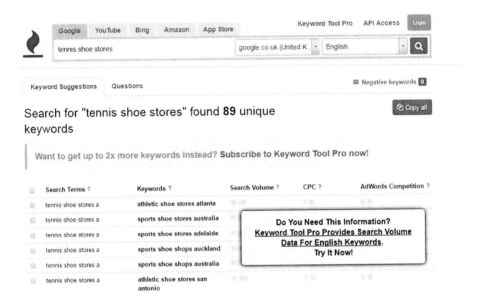

Figure 7-6. Keyword Tool at `http://keywordtool.io/`

Keywords generated include terms such as *athletic shoe stores*, *sports shoe shop Edmonton*, *exclusive tennis shoe stores*, and *top 10 athletic shoe stores*, to name a few. These terms can be copied to a clipboard and then pasted into Notepad or any CSV file list. Furthermore, you can upload the list to Google's Keyword Planner to see the search volume, CPC, and competition, which lets you narrow your search to terms that are most relevant and have high commercial value. This tool also has a commercial version called Keyword Tool Pro that lets you find more information such as the search volume, CPC, and AdWords competition.

In keyword research and strategy, what matters most is the type of words you use to streamline your website for users. For example, keywords such as *buy, buy now, Deal of the day, offers,* and *sale* are expected to lead to more conversions, whereas informative keywords like *How to, Free Download,* and *Installation procedure* do not help with conversions. You need to consider the conversion potential and commercial user intent before deciding which keywords to use.

Sizing Up the Competition

Your marketing strategy should always take your competitors into consideration before any implementation. Similarly, there are sites that can help you gain information about your competitors when you're doing keyword research. The best tools on the market for comprehensively gauging your competitors' tactics and keyword strategies are SpyFu and SEMrush.

SpyFu

SpyFu is a handy utility for keyword research: it is a comprehensive data mine that can help you gain insight into the statistics of your competitors. You can find out details of their organic searches, paid searches, and inbound links from Google (both organic and paid). You can also get statistics for keywords reflected on the first page, top organic competitors, top paid competitors, shared organic and paid keywords, AdWords history, organic ranking history, and domain strength of the competitors' sites.

As you can see in Figure 7-7, you can mine imperative metrics that can help you understand a significant bit about your competition's keyword strategies, results, and game-changing tactics. More information can be found at https://www.spyfu.com/.

Figure 7-7. *Sample report snapshot in SpyFu*

SEMrush

SEMrush is a utility that helps you delve deeper into keyword strategies, similar to SpyFu. From organic and paid searches, backlinks, referring domains, and organic keyword distribution to main competitor analysis, top anchors, and full-fledged reports, this toolset is a gold mine for SEO keyword strategies. Figure 7-8 shows a snapshot of an analysis of a site on the SEMrush interface. More Information on can be found at https://www.semrush.com/.

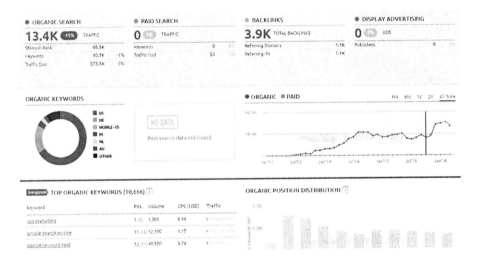

Figure 7-8. *Snapshot of an SEMrush analysis*

MozBar

MozBar is one of the best utilities when it comes to checking domain authority. You can check your site's domain authority, page authority, and spam score, including Facebook and Google+ activity. You can install a MozBar extension for Firefox and Google Chrome. For example, if you go to the Wikipedia home page, you can view the metrics on the MozBar strip interface, as shown in Figure 7-9.

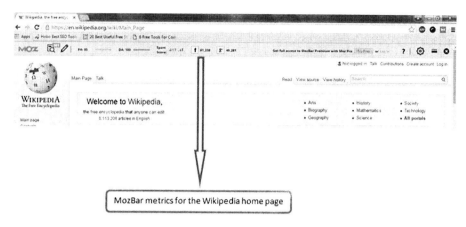

Figure 7-9. *MozBar metrics on the Wikipedia home page on Google Chrome*

In addition to these metrics, you can view link analysis metrics from an SEO perspective. You can also check the metrics for your competitors' sites and find out more about the referring domains, affiliate links, and domain authority for rival websites.

SEOquake

The SEOquake utility is an add-on that works with Firefox and Google Chrome. You can not only determine the page rank but also find information such as internal and external links and keyword density. You can perform a mini audit related to On-page factors and learn crucial information about two-word, three-word, and four-word phrases. Figure 7-10 shows a SEOquake overview of the Wikipedia home page.

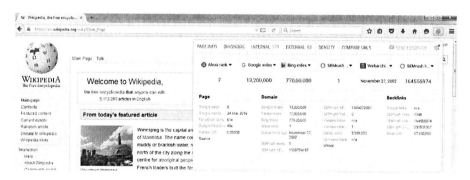

Figure 7-10. *SEOquake overview stats for Wikipedia*

Clicking the various tabs, such as Page Info, Diagnosis, and Compare URLs, leads to a fast audit of your website. Similar to MozBar, you can learn about your competitors' metrics and plan a strategy after gaining insight into the competition's keywords and other SEO-based tactics. Figure 7-11 shows the stats for Wikipedia using SEOquake.

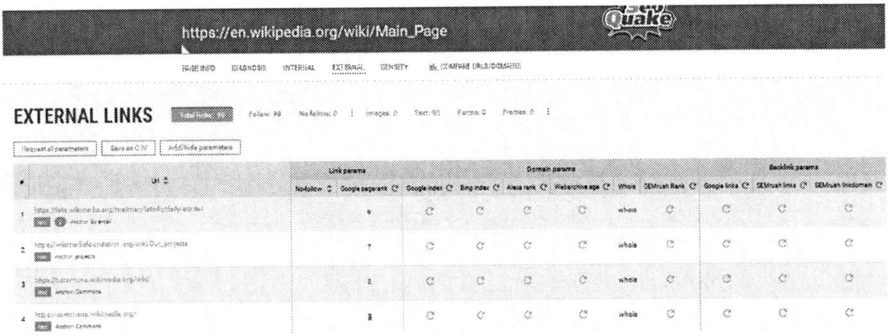

Figure 7-11. SEOquake External Link stats for Wikipedia

Boosting Your On-Page SEO Using Keywords and Long-Tail Terms

Once you prepare a list of keywords and phrases, the next step is to implement the list of keywords on your site. The following points suggest some ways to implement keywords as part of your on-page SEO process:

- *Title tags* educate the search engines about the web page and are important from a SEO perspective. Ensure that you have a keyword at the beginning or near the middle of your title tag. Also be sure each page has its own title tag. You can also enter synonyms or related words that have less competition but have strong potential for conversion optimization and streamlining the title tag. For example, *tennis shoes* has high competition and spans a huge range. Instead, you can use something like *tennis footwear and accessories,* which has less competition. Moreover, this kind of a long-tail term not only covers tennis shoes but also attracts attention for accessories usually associated with tennis equipment.

- *Do not stuff keywords into the title tag.* For example, if you are in the real estate sector in Toronto, stuffing similar keywords for your niche repeatedly in the title tag will be considered spammy by the search engines. An example of keyword stuffing in a title tag is as follows: *Real Estate: Homes sale, House sale, Real Estate Sale, Sale real estate Toronto.* On the other hand, here is a streamlined keyword-containing title tag: *Toronto, Real Estate & Homes for Sale, XYZ Realtors.* From the SEO perspective, the first example is spammy because it uses too many of the same or similar terms in one line in an attempt to manipulate and fool the search engines. The second example is crisp and concise, and mentions *Toronto* as the location, *Real Estate & Homes for Sale,* and the name *XYZ Realtors.*

- *Include keywords in the content on the page.* You can use a maximum of 2-3 keywords or related terms in the content. Remember, the content should be relevant and informative for the user. For example, if you are writing a blog on tennis shoes, you can include *tennis shoes* or its synonyms (such as *athletic tennis sneakers* and *cross trainers*) in the content. Be sure you do not stuff the content with keywords, or your site will be penalized by the search engines.

- Studies suggest that the *initial part of a page's content* is more likely to be mapped and stored by the search engines than content at the end.

- Use *short sentences,* and *wrap text around media* such as infographics, videos, and images. Interactive content with captions and image text containing relevant keywords or related terms are rated more due to its user-engaging paradigm. Using just text is boring and does not attract users. With search engines evolving, along with their ability to understand interactive media, it is important to make optimal use of interactive content along with relevant keywords for better results leading to higher rankings in the search results.

- *Using keywords in your Heading tags* can also streamline your On-page SEO efforts. If your page has a lot of sections, it is a good practice to use Heading tags. Start with Heading 1 (<h1>) tags and use Heading 2 and Heading 3 (<h2> and <h3>, respectively) for subsections. Make optimal use of relevant keywords in the content between these tags. As mentioned earlier, do not stuff Headings with too many or irrelevant keywords, to avoid a penalty. For Heading 2 and Heading 3 tags, use synonyms or alternative text keywords so that the search engines understand that the content is relevant and has a good workflow.

- If possible, *incorporate keywords or relevant synonyms in the URLs and internal content*. Given how competitive SEO is, most URLs are already taken. However, you can use relevant keywords if such a URL is available. Use specific keywords in your anchor text if possible. The keywords should be distinct and not generic so that the search engines can establish that the keywords are relevant and used appropriately.

Summary

Keywords are an integral part of the SEO process and are important for your campaigns. You should do plenty of research and not be too manipulative, keeping in mind that user intent and satisfaction are prime and more important than stuffing in keywords or over optimizing to befool the search engines. The next chapter looks at link building, which is the core of every SEO project.

CHAPTER 8

▓ ▓ ▓

Link Building

Link building is a methodology that results in getting external pages of another site to point to your website. They may be links from a blog, affiliates, or any relevant source. Inbound links help search engines understand the popularity of a site and hence are important.

Because each inbound link to a site results in a SEO boost for that website, the link enhances the rankings significantly. Unfortunately, at one time, SEO experts misused the power of this factor and advocated using underhanded techniques to manipulate the SERPs, such as *link farming*, which included many external sites pointing to a site that had no relevance to the page. In other words, links from hundreds of sites pointed to the target site just to boost the SEO rankings for that site. As a result, Google in particular cracked down on this behavior and introduced penalties, because these tactics defeat the purpose of users getting relevant and meaningful information in their search results. However, getting links from other sites is a major ranking factor and is crucial to the SEO process of any site. Thus the new concept of follow and no-follow links was established.

Follow links are considered by the search engines and result in higher page rankings. On the other hand, *no-follow links* are not considered valuable by Google and other search engines and so are of little consequence in getting a SEO boost.

For example, the reference section in Wikipedia was used to promote personal sites, leading to irrelevant links. Therefore, Wikipedia assigned the no-follow method to the reference section to dissuade people from using the Wikipedia platform for black-hat techniques. But you need to remember that no-follow links are not worthless—if the links are genuine and keep user intent in mind, they can still result in substantial traffic for a site, thereby opening up opportunities for boosting site rankings. If the links are useful, users will check out and recommend your site, resulting in effective traffic. Referral traffic is valuable, if you consider the user perspective. So, you cannot totally discount the effect of no-follow links when it comes to SEO implementation.

Generally, SEO experts recommend a natural link profile with a healthy balance of follow and no-follow links as well as domain authority for boosting your SEO process.

Important Factors for Link Building

This section looks at the factors that play a role in link building. Rather than focusing on quantity, link building is more quality based. Before you delve into how to get quality links, you need to understand what these factors are and why they are crucial from a SEO perspective.

© Aravind Shenoy and Anirudh Prabhu 2016
A. Shenoy and A. Prabhu, *Introducing SEO*, DOI 10.1007/978-1-4842-1854-9_8

Relevance

Relevance is imperative for link building. For example, suppose you have a website that caters to the plumbing business. Links from external sites catering to flooring businesses, plumbing equipment, and plumbing wikis carry more weight than links from irrelevant sites that focus on tourists, flights, hotels, and so on. The search engines are getting smarter and understand relevance better than in earlier days. Google and the other search engines value relevance and topic-specific link building more than most of the other SEO factors.

Localization is another relevant attribute. For example, links from plumbing equipment manufacturers in London are more relevant to a plumbing site in London than plumbing equipment manufacturers in California.

Trustworthiness and Popularity

Link building takes into account the reliability and popularity of external websites that point toward your site. For example, if your site is related to software development or web design, links from domains such as Stack Overflow have more weight than newly built sites.

Social Media Links

Getting inbound links from social media platforms is a given and no longer an option. At one time, social media platforms such as Facebook and Twitter were not given much importance; but with the advent of social networking, this has evolved into a crucial factor. You cannot overlook the social media platform.

For example, a link from a product page on Facebook to an e-commerce site hosting similar products definitely helps and also increases your site's visibility to a large audience. Another example is links from sites such as Zomato, Foursquare, or TripAdvisor pointing toward a restaurant or hotel site, thus increasing traffic significantly.

Interactive Content

Although text is important, nowadays content is based more on intuitive and interactive media such as infographics, videos, and images. Links from external pages with efficient media content result in more traffic for your website and are certainly a driving factor for link building. For example, suppose you have a site that sells computer peripherals and hardware. Sites that contain tips and troubleshooting videos for computer peripherals are preferable and fun to watch, in addition to being informative. Therefore, links from these sites result in more traffic and are very important from a user perspective.

Spamming

Links from spammy sites are a definite no-no because they result in penalties. For example, a site with adware or malware is disturbing to users. Search engines quickly sniff out these sites, and if your sites receive links from such sites, your site's SERPs will suffer.

Another spammy behavior is flooding your pages with inbound links from irrelevant sources in an effort to make your site popular. Eventually the search engines will figure out this deceit. You can even be delisted from the SERPs.

Domain Authority

Domain authority is an important factor in link building. Sites such as Stack Overflow have been in business for a decade. Therefore, these sites have a higher reliability quotient—but that's not all. Most popular domains have existed for quite a while and are linked to relevant sites. The link juice spread by these domains is handy because these sites have established themselves.

Studies suggest that a new website receiving backlinks from an authoritative site is more visible and may rank earlier in the SERPs compared to sites receiving links from unknown sites. In addition, being linked to malware-infested sites can result in your site being delisted from the SERPs; but if a site like Stack Overflow or Quora receives inbound links from spammy sites, it holds its own.

░ **Tip** Remember the follow and no-follow attributes explained earlier in the chapter. Your site can get substantial referral traffic even if the no-follow attribute is assigned by site owners and moderators of these trustworthy portals.

User-Engaging Content

Your link's popularity is also based on the informative content found on your website. If the content is top-notch, bloggers, influencers, and subject matter experts will link to your site. For example, people link to Stack Overflow for troubleshooting tips and informative articles. Such websites are often referred to and therefore are considered more reliable due to their user-engaging content.

Link and Content Freshness

Another aspect is the freshness of links. If the information on your site and the links to your site were created a long time ago, there is little user engagement. Freshness of links and page content is a prime factor in link building. You can always create new links and keep your content updated to receive more links from people in your niche industry.

For example, Zurb Foundation 6 is the latest release by the founders of the framework. If your site has informative content about Zurb Foundation 4, fewer people are going to link to it, because it is an outdated version and is rarely used. However, if you update the content to Zurb Foundation 6 and introduce new links for people to access that content, more people will link to your site due to its freshness and up-to-date content.

Link-Building Resources and Utilities

Now that you have seen the major link-building factors, you understand the resources that can optimize your link building and lead to higher traffic, resulting in more leads and eventually higher revenue for your organization. Although many SEO experts suggest using a mix of white-hat, black-hat, and grey-hat techniques for link building, it is better to steer away from black-hat and grey-hat techniques because they are bound to be discovered and lead to penalties from the search engines (especially Google). We only discusses white-hat techniques, because we believe that doing research and not being manipulative is the key to SEO success.

This section looks at the following resources that can result in maximum optimization of your link-building strategies:

- Content-based strategy

- E-mail outreach campaigns

- Guest posting methods

- Forums, RSS feeds, and blogging

- Social media, social bookmarking, and web directories

- Networking with influencers and subject matter experts

- Competitor-based research

Content-Based Strategy

Relevant content is king, and any SEO implementation is incomplete without user-engaging content. If your content is top-notch, it may be what users are looking for. Use interactive media such as infographics and videos in your page content. Enable users and readers to embed that content in their web pages and blogs, which will link back to your site.

Use innovative words that are unique and catchy, thereby building up a persona for your site and the team behind it. Hold user-engaging contests and include contextual deals in your content. For example, if your site is into renting out musical instruments, hold contests and post quizzes that reach out to a large user base.

If your site is an informative one, build up tutorials and learning videos to engage users positively. Moderate the reviews and answer customers' queries on your website so you're in sync with users and show that you care. Use Google Hangouts and other tools, such as Skype, to connect with users for a better UX. This approach encourages customers and users to link to your site and will increase traffic significantly. Keep your customers updated about the latest products, and ask them to link back to your site, thereby increasing interaction.

E-mail Outreach Campaigns

Although some SEO experts are skeptical about e-mail outreach methods, they are an awesome way to get backlinks. Create outstanding templates that are catchy and creative in addition to using power-pitched content.

Find broken links on your target sites using tools such as Open Site Explorer, and approach the sites' webmasters. Once you tell them about the broken links, you can request via e-mail that they replace those links with links to your site or, even better, use the same anchor text to link back to similar content on your site. If the content is good enough and fresh, there is a higher probability that the sites' webmasters will link back to the sites using those very links. Interact with and give suggestions to the webmasters of those sites regarding techniques that can boost their SEO. Ask them to backlink to your website. If your site has informative content, you can list the benefits and encourage the target site's webmaster to link back to the site. For example, contacting web design–based education sites to link back to the basic tutorials on your site that will encourage them to backlink to your site.

You can find a plethora of e-mail templates on the web that you can customize and send to your prospective audience. As mentioned, SEO experts argue about the viability of e-mail outreach, but these tactics work on a micro level and you may get a good response from people in your niche industry.

We recommend the templates for an e-mail outreach campaigns found on the Quick Sprout website by Neil Patel, who is a subject matter expert in the industry. The following link points to an extremely handy guide: https://www.quicksprout.com/2012/12/07/the-link-builders-guide-to-e-mail-outreach/.

Guest-Posting Methods

Guest posting is definitely an opportunity that you do not want to overlook in your link building strategies. Find out the target audience and prospective readers for your guest posts. You can use search strings such as *(Your Keyword/s) + Guest Posts, (Y your Keyword/s) + Submit Posts, (Your Keyword/s) + Blogger posts,* and *(Your Keywords) + Tips and Troubleshooting guest blogs,* to name a few. Figure 8-1 shows an example.

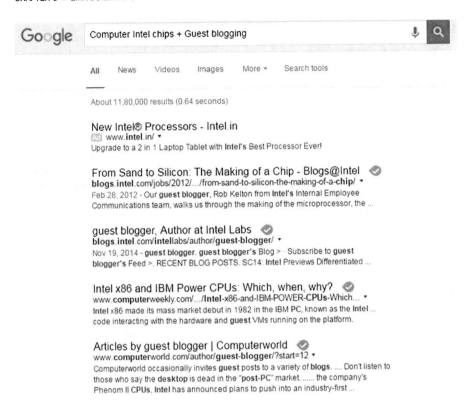

Figure 8-1. *Intel chips guest blogging results*

Figure 8-1 shows the keywords *Computer intel chips* with the term *guest blogging*. The results can help you sniff out opportunities where you can post guest comments.

Use Google, Twitter, and Pinterest to find the latest guest posts and interactive content along with tweets, which throw open a host of possibilities for guest posts. You can locate guest posts by other authors, which will help you locate guest-post opportunities for that niche. Once you get the information, start guest posting on those avenues. Acknowledge tweets or comments from other guest authors and send requests to them to backlink to your site. You can even sneak a link to your website into those guest posts. Just be sure you don't post anything that is not relevant or not contextual. For example, you can type in the link of your advanced HTML tutorials in a guest post on a web design education site. You can also throw in troubleshooting code errors, tips and tricks to enhance the HTML code, or links to videos that explain the designing aspect, prompting backlinks from the intended audience.

Guest posting on authority domains is supposed to have a better chance of acquiring backlinks. For example, troubleshooting tips about CSS styles for coding errors on Stack Overflow can get you more backlinks from prospective readers and subject matter experts from the web design industry, who are always looking for solutions to problems. Introducing a backlink in your posts or sending requests to the target audience is a good way to acquire backlinks.

Forums, RSS Feeds, and Blogging

Forums and online communities are an excellent way to build rapport with like-minded professionals. Be active and participate in questions and answers, include your suggestions on the topic at hand, conduct online discussions, and try to become a reliable source of information for users. Be relevant, and do not try to spam the forums, because spamming will lead to your site being delisted by the forum moderators. Once you are accepted by forum users as a go-to person for those topics, you can request a link back to your site. Do not over-optimize on forums, and be appreciative of any good forum posting because it can expand your network significantly.

RSS feeds are another excellent utility for link building. If users use the content on your site, you can ask them for a link back to your site's pages. Wordpress and other CMS platforms have the RSS feed facility, and using extensions and plug-ins, you can ensure that a link is added to your blog for every post. Submit your RSS feeds to RSS directories such as Blogdigger, FeedListing, and RSSFeeds.org for more exposure, resulting in link juice for your feeds that are linked to sections of your posts.

Blogging is also an important factor in getting link juice for your site. You can respond to topic-specific content in third-party blogs and eventually expand your network. You can create user-engaging blogs for various products. Create blogs not only for your site but also for other users, and trade links with them. Reach out and pass links to reliable blogs that are specific to your niche; this will help you build good rapport with people in your community, following which you can ask for a backlink to your site. Submit your blog to directories such as Blogdigger for more link juice and exposure. Create useful blogs for engaging content such as "Top Fashion Trends in 2016" or "15 tips and tricks to get the most out of your SEO Keyword strategies" or "Top 20 Hotels in London," depending on your niche.

Blogging is all about credibility and reliability. Once you have a foothold in the blogs for your niche or related product categories, you can expect more links to your site in a natural way. (You always get what you give.)

Social Media, Social Bookmarking, and Web Directories

Social media, social bookmarking, and web directories are also potential sources for link building. Social media platforms can be used for links for your site or advertising your products and services. You can build rapport with like-minded professionals via conversations on Twitter. Word-of-mouth publicity from users through portals such as Facebook and Google+ can be excellent for your business, and users will link back to your site. Connect with users using Google Hangouts, and reply to their reviews or feedback.

Promote surveys and feedback forms on social media sites. You can send discount coupons or deals using sites such as Groupon and, at the same time, use anchor text in them that point to your site. You can take advantage of the benefits of Reddit and Pinterest to further your cause in your niche. Building brand awareness is also possible through these platforms, and users will link back to your site depending on product quality and their UX.

Web directories are handy when it comes to link building. You can benefit from their exposure (although it is less than that of social media) and use a backlink to your site. There are several web directories specific to various categories or niches. Advertising your site or brand on these directories is useful, and backlinks in the directories to your site or product pages may result in more link juice.

Networking with Influencers and Subject Matter Experts

Influencers and subject matter experts (SMEs) are a vital cog in the wheel for your link-building process. Build a rapport by initially contacting them through portals such as LinkedIn. You can also respond to their Twitter tweets (make sure your tweets and responses are credible and genuine). Interact with them on forums and in specific online communities. Contribute and give suggestions in your niche.

For example, explaining certain things (such as troubleshooting framework issues, explaining coding techniques, or recommending software development tools) on Stack Overflow or answering topic-specific queries (such as which programming language is the best for creating an e-commerce platform) on Quora can help a lot in social networking. E-mail outreach using catchy e-mails is another way of communicating with them.

These people have a certain authority in their niche, so you need to be sure your communication with them is relevant and straight to the point. Do not use kiddy measures such as responding to every tweet or response, which may backfire. Your approach should be meaningful, and you need to really earn your links with these experts.

Cover topics that can be of use to readers in your niche category, and leave insightful comments or videos that can actually be good resources for readers to prove your reliability. Send links to the blogs of these influencers when users want information related to your niche or product category. Collaborate with experts in prelaunch events and promotions, and gain credibility through social traction. Be authentic and not pushy. Subscribe to their RSS feeds and create good content to further your cause. Eventually, you can ask them for backlinks to your pages that are relevant to the products or services and ask them for recommendations and suggestions.

Competitor-Based Research

Competitor-based research is always necessary when it comes to effective link building. You can find out what backlinks are received by your competitors and save those interactions to analyze the prospective audience and user groups. You can also learn about their partners or affiliates in that niche.

Competitors have people who work with them and supply goods or services. Find out more about these indirect competitors. Consider an example of a plumbing business. Plumbing-related items such as water taps and pipes are supplied by manufacturers for your plumbing competitors. By connecting with the manufacturers, you can gain more exposure and ask them to recommend your business by providing backlinks to your site.

Also remember that localization plays an important role. You can learn more about your competitors' business in your vicinity, such as those offering plumbing services. Connect with authors who have recommended your competitors or engaged with them over their products or services. Once you establish a connection by using online surveys, forums, social media, or e-mails, you can send a request to those authors to review your products, recommend your business, or share reviews and point toward your business using backlinks.

Link-Building Tools

Many toolsets can help you streamline your link-building efforts, including SEOquake, MozBar, Open Site Explorer, Rmoov, and Majestic SEO. Chapter 7 (related to keyword strategies and research) gave you an overview of SEOquake and MozBar, and Chapter 10 (which focuses on utilities and tools used in SEO implementation) covers Open Site Explorer, Rmoov, and Majestic SEO.

This section covers the following utilities:

- OpenLinkProfiler

- Alltop

- Flickr

OpenLinkProfiler

OpenLinkProfiler is a free tool used for in-depth analysis of backlinks. You can get data on the freshest backlinks to your site (including the complete set of backlinks). You can download exactly 1,000 in a CSV format. With customized link-filtering and link-disinfection attributes, this can be a handy utility in your link-building strategy.

- Figure 8-2 shows a backlink analysis snapshot using OpenLinkProfiler. (Wikipedia is the site being analyzed for backlinks.) You can find more information at http://openlinkprofiler.org/.

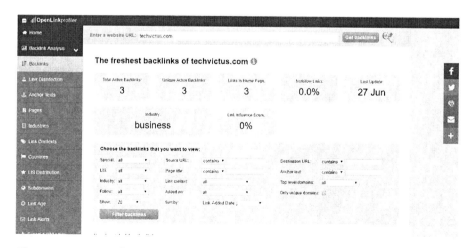

Figure 8-2. OpenLinkProfiler

Alltop

Alltop enables you to start networking with influencers, SMEs, and hardcore professionals prior to undertaking your link-building process. Figure 8-3 shows a snapshot of influencers and professionals in their respective niches.

Figure 8-3. *Alltop*

You can create a personal online hub for your favorite blogs and sites. Using Alltop's Feeds functionality, you can receive e-mails and alerts about the latest updates and posts on your favorite sites and blogs. Using this utility, you can be the first person to comment on those posts. This networking ability helps you build relationships with prospective influencers. You can reach out to SMEs who regularly create posts on their blogs or sites and develop a rapport with them, eventually coaxing them to link back to your site if the site has good, relevant content in their niche. More information can be found at http://alltop.com/.

Flickr

Flickr (https://www.flickr.com) is a photo and video sharing and hosting site with a large, vibrant community (see Figure 8-4). When you upload images or videos to Flickr, you can add a link in the description to gain credit for that media. This method can get you real, genuine backlinks. Alternatively, you can use Google Images search (https://images.google.com) or TinEye (https://www.tineye.com) for a reverse image search and locate sites that are using your video or image. You can request a backlink from them if they have not done so already.

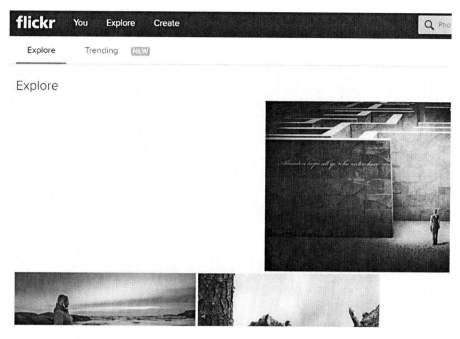

Figure 8-4. *Flickr*

Another important use of Flickr is finding potential users and SMEs in your industry. Initially, locate images and videos in your niche. You can then use a backlink analysis tool to find pages linked to those images. This way, you can reach out to professionals in your niche who are using these images on their sites. This is a potentially great resource for reaching out to a wider audience. It not only expands your social-networking scope but also sheds lights on leads that can result in more traffic on your site and, eventually, more sales and revenue.

Summary

This chapter looked at important factors and resources for link building. You also took a look at unconventional tools such as Flickr and Alltop, which can be used for link prospecting. The next chapter explores content consideration and its impact on SEO.

CHAPTER 9

Content Considerations

Content plays a major role in your SEO strategy. Creating engaging content is extremely important because it results in users being glued to your website. You need to remember that users use the power of search engines to search and locate content that is relevant and meaningful. Therefore, the purpose of SEO content is to provide meaningful information based on users' search queries. It is important that while writing content, you think about users and not search engines: first write good, user-engaging content, and then tweak it for better visibility.

For example, suppose you have an informative website related to troubleshooting Windows 7 systems. You need to ensure that your content actually helps users repair and remove errors from their Windows 7 OS. Once you write troubleshooting tips and tricks for resolving several issues, you can then tweak the content by introducing keywords. But remember not to stuff keywords or over-optimize the content, because that will result in penalties from Google and the other search engines.

Content Consideration Factors and Subsequent Implementation

Let's look at the essential factors when you are considering content and how to achieve efficient SEO implementation on your site.

Relevance

Writing meaningful content is the most important factor in content creation. The evolution of search engines was to help users find out information they need and it is all about creating an efficient user experience. The content should be crisp and meaningful to engage users. If the content is thin (meaning it is of less value from the user's perspective or so commonplace that it is not useful to readers), then you will see a huge bounce rate (because users will not stay on a site that's of no value to them), thereby adversely affecting the site's rankings. You can streamline your content once it is written by using a calculated (not manipulative) and creative approach. Ensure that users get valuable information on your web pages, which will encourage them to share or recommend your site and thus enhance the site's visibility.

© Aravind Shenoy and Anirudh Prabhu 2016
A. Shenoy and A. Prabhu, *Introducing SEO*, DOI 10.1007/978-1-4842-1854-9_9

You also need to consider the appropriate target audience when you publish content. Using Google Analytics, you can gauge your prospective and existing audience. Catering to the correct audience makes you content more relevant. An investor is more likely to view content about Wall Street than web designers. On the other hand, a site displaying content about troubleshooting website design errors is more likely to be viewed by web designers and UX designers than investment bankers.

For example, suppose you want to buy shoes online for a party in Denver, Colorado. You go to an e-commerce site such as Amazon do so. The product description for a shoe should tell you about its comfort, style, materials, price, sole, and so on. If the description primarily includes content about plumbing solutions in Alaska, it will be a huge turnoff, because it will be of no use to you and is misleading. This is spam advertising and can harm the site's reputation due to deceitful marketing. You may end up never visiting that site again.

Keyword Positioning

Remember that once you write content, you can tweak it for maximum optimization. However, you need to find appropriate keywords that do justice to the content. You can include a keyword in the first line or heading and then use synonyms in the next paragraph. But do not include a keyword if it is not relevant.

Studies suggest that search engines prefer to map keywords that appear in the initial portion of the content than later in the web page. So, try to include a keyword or key phrase in the first few paragraphs of the page to position it better so it can be mapped easily by the search engines

Headings and Subheadings

Use headings and subheadings to give your content a concise structure. Heading elements help to organize your content. Insert keywords or related terms in the headings, because they are cached easily. Search engines prefer keywords to be included in headings because they are topic-specific and the hierarchy helps users locate and access content. Having a structured format such as a heading, body, and conclusion also makes your site more readable.

Outbound Links

When you're writing topic-specific content, link jargon (industry-specific words) and buzzwords to authoritative sites. For example, if you are writing about web design, topic-specific words can be linked to sites like Stack Overflow.

Suppose your site is a travel website where users can rent hotels, cars, and tour packages in Australia. Koalas and kangaroos can be sighted frequently in certain places in Australia. If users are ignorant about animals such as koalas, you can link the word *koalas* to the appropriate Wikipedia page. Such links make your site seem reliable and genuine and help provide a good UX.

Lists and Fonts

If users want to view troubleshooting steps for their operating system, a site displaying paragraphs of text and numbers will be boring and tedious to read. However, if you specify the troubleshooting steps using numbered bullets, it helps users by giving them concise, specific instructions to resolve their system issues. Instead of writing a comprehensive paragraph explaining all the steps, use lists; for example, something like "Top 10 resources for Windows 7 troubleshooting" is useful, and users may recommend or share your site on social media and other platforms.

Also consider using bold fonts and italics on your web page. Keywords can be assigned a bold font or italics style to help the search engines map those terms and relevant information. But take care that you do not over-optimize too many terms on a single page, because that can be ambiguous for the search engines.

You can also use alternate text for listings, images, and videos. It helps the search engines map appropriately and gives the relevance.

Proofreading and Plagiarism

Before you publish content on your website, be sure you have edited and proofread it. Spelling and grammatical errors can be an absolute turn-off and reflect poorly on the quality of your site, thereby adversely affecting the rankings. Sentence structure issues can also result in a negative experience for users. They may even doubt the authenticity of the site, which can affect your site's reputation.

Remember to check your site for plagiarism. Search engines penalize sites that have copied content from other sites. Your content must be original and specific from the user's perspective. You can use plagiarism tools such as Copyscape to deal with this issue.

High-Quality, Intuitive Content

The most important factor is to publish quality content. Quality matters, and using sharp, intelligent content will lead to good results. For example, informative blogs are in vogue, because they supplement the main product and educate users about various aspects of the product.

Use interactive media such as videos, audio, and infographics to engage users and increase the popularity of your website. Use social media plug-ins and links so that users can share your content or recommend it to other users. Compress images for optimal page-load times.

Be as informative as possible, but keep in mind that the length of your content matters. It is a good practice to have a word count of approximately 250–300 on a single web page. Depending on the type of site, you can also use 800–900 word articles that provide in-depth information. It also helps to include a few key terms to enhance your SEO implementation.

Generate fresh content for your users, because freshness is a key SEO factor. Users are not interested in redundant, stale content; they want to read the latest and are always on the lookout for trendy updates.

Tools Used for Content Consideration and Curation

When it comes to content consideration and curation, many toolsets and utilities are available for the SEO and digital marketing industry. You can use the power of these utilities to acquire and provide the latest information on your site.

Digg

Digg is a news aggregator that provides compelling content and caters to a global audience (see Figure 9-1). It has articles and news related to ongoing trends, caters to several categories, and is powered by social signals. It is an abundant source of information, and you can find the latest and most relevant updates in any genre here. You can find more information at http://digg.com/.

Figure 9-1. Digg

Quora

Quora (www.quora.com) is a questions-and-answers website where you can find views and reviews for almost any niche (see Figure 9-2). It is a platform that acts like a blog, forums, social media, and wikis and that caters to a widespread community. Its reach and unique content are useful; for example, the questions in Quora resemble search queries and hence can be used as long-tail terms. The community-based approach, with industry experts sharing information, is a bank of content in itself.

Figure 9-2. *Quora*

LinkedIn Pulse

LinkedIn Pulse (`www.linkedin.com/pulse`) is LinkedIn's blogging platform (see Figure 9-3).
Creating a blog requires the ability to write; but, more important, blogging builds up a
wide audience. LinkedIn Pulse helps you connect with a large audience in addition to
categorizing and sharing your content; in particular, you can build a network with subject
matter experts (SMEs) and influencers in your niche. You can also keep your users
engaged by posting fresh content on a regular basis.

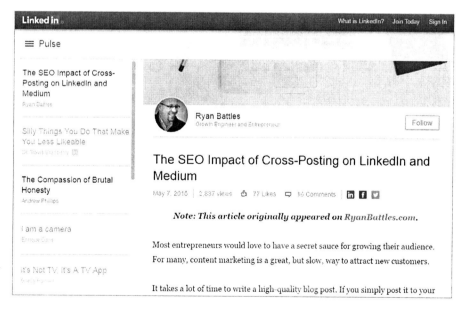

Figure 9-3. *LinkedIn Pulse*

Copyscape

As mentioned earlier, Copyscape is a plagiarism-checking tool that looks for duplicate or copied content (see Figure 9-4). It provides information about URLs that have words matching content found on the web.

Figure 9-4. Copyscape

Although it offers additional premium services such as daily scanning for content copied from your site and sending plagiarism banners to potential plagiarists, the plagiarism checker is free to use. You can determine which content is redundant and used on sites across the web. To access this tool, go to www.copyscape.com.

Summary

This chapter looked at factors that affect content consideration and strategy. You learned about some common tools that can help you consider and select content.

The next chapter gives you an overview of tools and utilities used for keyword research, deep site crawling, link building and analysis, site speed, content building and optimization, and site audits.

CHAPTER 10

▓ ▓ ▓

SEO Hub: Utilities and Toolsets

A plethora of SEO Toolkits can help you check, manage, analyze, audit, and streamline your SEO projects. In earlier chapters, you looked at some Google utilities that can be used for SEO projects. You also gained a basic understanding of the different aspects of SEO. In a real-time scenario, you cannot check each and every factor to boost your SEO process.

To help you implement SEO quickly, you can use several tools. Some of them are freeware and open source; others offer a free trial or are commercial. This chapter looks at some of these tools, which can be handy in your SEO projects.

This overview presents SEO tools in the following categories:

- Keyword research and analysis

- Deep site crawlers

- Link building, link removal, and link analysis

- Site speed

- Content building and optimization

- Site audits

Keyword Research and Analysis

Many tools (both free and premium) can aid you in keyword research and analysis. You saw Google's Keyword Planner earlier in the book. This section look at several toolsets you can use to find appropriate and competitive keywords, long-tail phrases, and related analytics.

© Aravind Shenoy and Anirudh Prabhu 2016
A. Shenoy and A. Prabhu, *Introducing SEO*, DOI 10.1007/978-1-4842-1854-9_10

Soovle

Soovle is a handy utility that helps with keyword research and site optimization. It is tailored for small- and medium-size businesses that do not have the budget of enterprise-grade setups. You can generate suggestions from several search engines for keywords or long-tail terms, and you can analyze the performance and frequency of those keywords on multiple platforms including Google, Bing, Amazon, Answers, and Yahoo!. For information about this tool, go to www.soovle.com/.

WordStream

WordStream's tool suite has keyword suggestions, grouping, analysis, and negative keyword utilities baked in on its platform (see Figure 10-1). You can take advantage of these utilities to generate terms and analyze their potential. More information can be found at www.wordstream.com/free-keyword-tools.

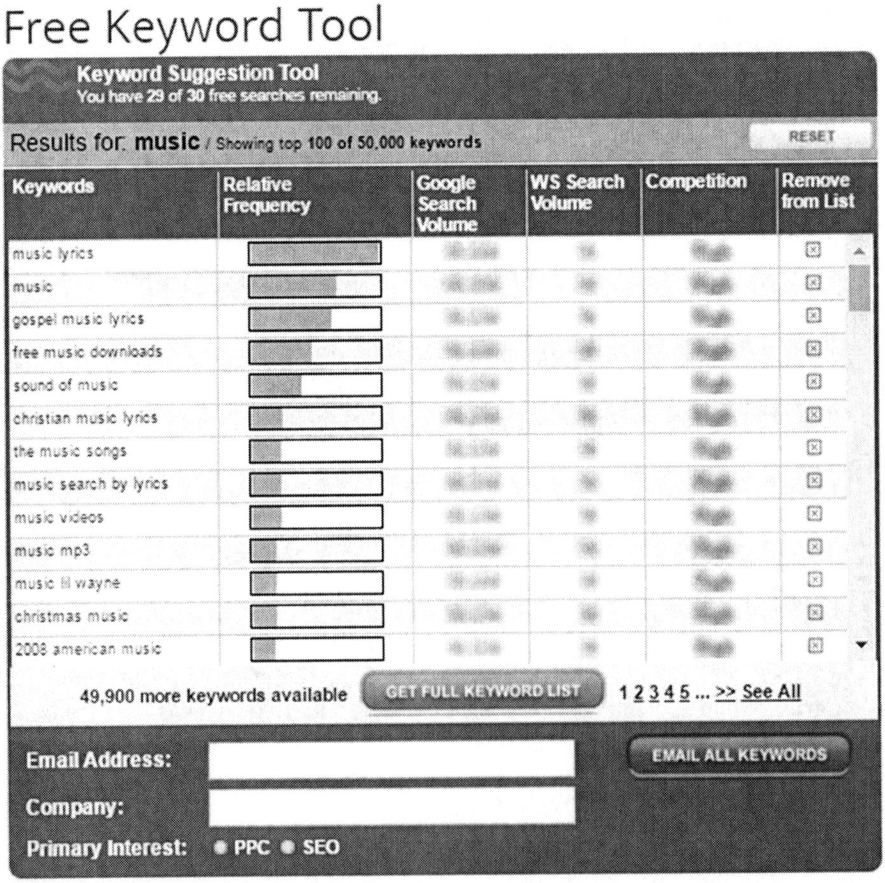

Figure 10-1. WordStream's Free Keyword Tool

Übersuggest

Übersuggest is batteries included, meaning you can not only search for potential keywords but also filter them by region (country-specific) and medium (such as Web, Images, and News). You can find this super tool at https://ubersuggest.io/. Figure 10-2 shows its interface and results.

Figure 10-2. *Übersuggest*

Deep Site Crawlers

Several crawler tools are available that can crawl your site's URLs and help you find bottlenecks and quickly identify technical and architectural issues. This indicates potential issues that may arise when a real-time search engine spider crawls through your site. You can also use these tools for SEO audits; doing so abstracts away the need to perform manual checks.

There are several kinds of free and commercial web crawler toolkits. The most popular are Screaming Frog, DeepCrawl, and Rob Hammond's SEO Crawler.

Screaming Frog Spider

Screaming Frog SEO Spider is a compact desktop application that crawls all the links, images, and CSS on a website to find flaws (see Figure 10-3). It helps you analyze different on-site attributes such as page titles, heading tags, external links, redirect chains, canonical elements, and images, to name a few.

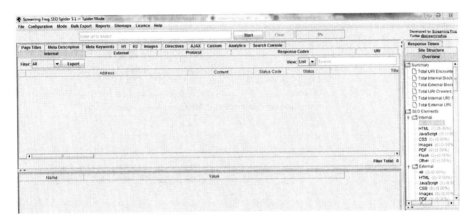

Figure 10-3. *Screaming Frog's desktop interface*

The Lite version is available for free and has a URL crawl limit of 500. You can also opt for the Premium version, which includes unlimited crawling, access to all configuration functionality, a custom code-search facility, and technical support. More info about this robust tool can be found at www.screamingfrog.co.uk/seo-spider/.

DeepCrawl

DeepCrawl is a commercial web-crawling tool with a cloud-based SaaS model where you can define the crawl depth, do custom URL rewrites, and compare reports (see Figure 10-4). You can schedule crawls, create tickets (with the ability to re-verify whether defects such as broken links have been fixed), and conduct a gap analysis in addition to crawling tons of pages. More information can be found at https://www.deepcrawl.com/.

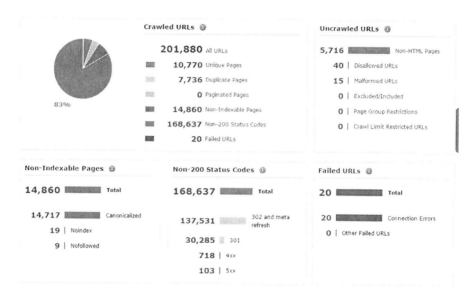

Figure 10-4. *Statistics on DeepCrawl*

DeepCrawl's heavy-lifting capabilities and premium report features (such as comparing your site reports with your competitors' report) make it a vital cog in the wheel for enterprise-grade websites.

SEO Crawler by Rob Hammond

SEO Crawler by Rob Hammond is an awesome free utility for deep crawling (see Figure 10-5). It is flexible, and there is no need to log in with your credentials to take advantage of this web-based toolkit. It runs on mobile devices and desktops alike, meaning you can check a site's behavior on different platforms, simulating the way desktop, tablet, and mobile bots crawl the site in a real-time scenario. It is useful for on-page optimization and helps you sort technical and architectural flaws on your site. You can find more information at `http://robhammond.co/tools/seo-crawler`.

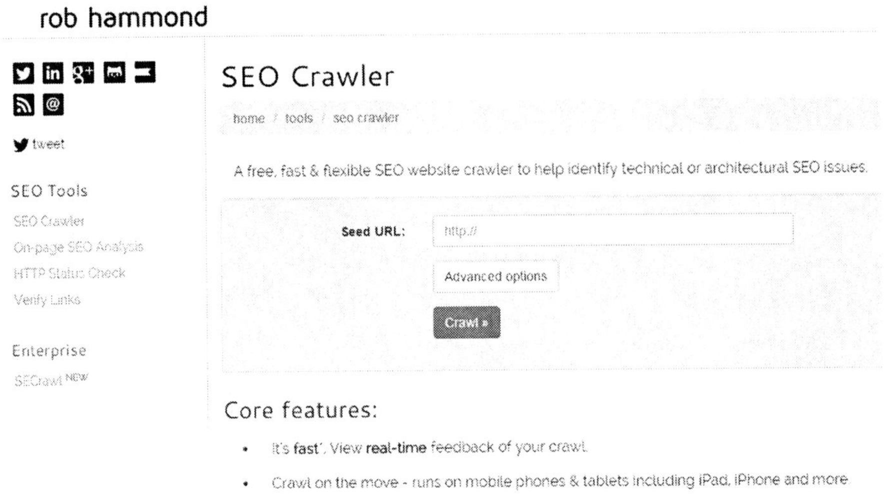

Figure 10-5. *Rob Hammond's SEO Crawler*

Link Building, Link Removal, and Link Analysis

Several types of link-focused tools cater to different functionalities such as analyzing backlinks, indicating spam links, link building, and broken-link checking.

Majestic SEO

With capabilities such as comprehensive checking of backlinks, link research, and link building, Majestic SEO is a premium tool that helps you gain insight into external backlinks, referring domains, referring IPs, and referring subnets (see Figure 10-6). You can find information such as sites that provide quality links and sites that link to your competitors, and gather link-building ideas. More information about this tool suite can be found at https://majestic.com/.

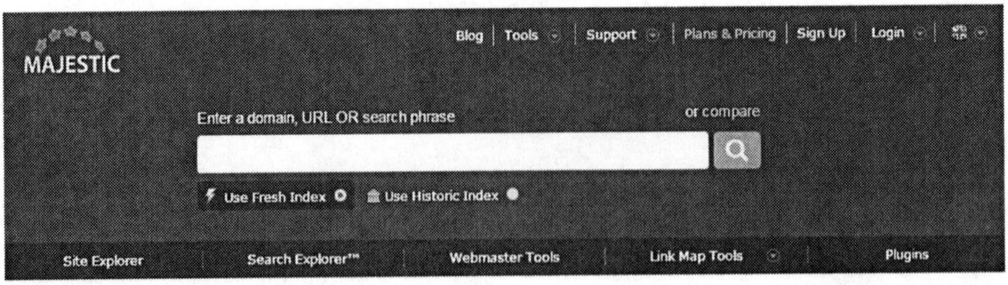

Figure 10-6. *Majestic SEO*

Open Site Explorer

The Open Site Explorer is one of the utilities present in the Moz ecosystem (https://moz.com/). It helps you track inbound links to your site and comes with features such as enhanced comparison metrics, finding broken links, social media-based links, and information about domain authority. You can learn about anchor text on other sites that point to your website, do spam analysis, find link opportunities, and generate advanced reports for analytics and strategies. You can also learn what type of content has helped your competitors to get inbound links and scale your link-building processes significantly.

This toolset also suggests missed-link opportunities, including potential mentions of your brand that are not currently linked. This tool also facilitates the process of exporting link research and analysis data in Excel format, and it supports visual tracking by displaying statistics in pie charts. This systematic and highly organized utility is a vital cog in the wheel for link building and research and can streamline your digital marketing campaign processes. You can find more information at https://moz.com/researchtools/ose/. Figure 10-7 shows the interface of the Open Site Explorer tool.

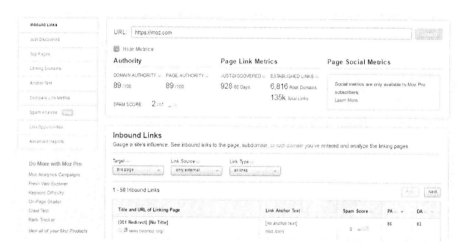

Figure 10-7. *Open Site Explorer*

Rmoov

Inbound links are a crucial factor in SEO. However, inbound links should be relevant and from popular, safe domains. Inbound links from spammy websites and questionable sources can result in penalties from Google and other search engines. In order to fix these problems, you need to generate a list of spammy URLs and then address it to Google by using Google's Disavow tool. (For more information on the Google Disavow tool, see the article at https://support.google.com/webmasters/answer/2648487.)

At some point your site may be penalized, and you need to send a reconsideration request to Google. Enter Rmoov: a handy utility that auto-generates reports that can be uploaded to Google's Disavow tool. This utility helps you contact domain owners and sends them a link-disavow request. You can also send reconsideration requests to Google if you are penalized. This link-pruning tool also ensures that spam links are cleaned up and records every step you take in a Google doc, helping you stay in sync with the latest link-pruning actions performed on your site. This site has a free version as well as an enhanced commercial version that can help you remove low-quality and bad links, thereby detoxing your site. You can find more information at www.rmoov.com. Figure 10-8 shows the Rmoov Domain Editor.

rmoov Domain Editor ♥

Website Owner	⚠ ☑ DB Lookup
Whois Email	⊙ Do not link check this
Secondary Email	⊙ No Whois Email Availa
Owner Address	☑ No Secondary Email A
Owner Address More	
Owner City/St/Zip	
Owner Country	
Owner Phone	
Owner Twitter	
Owner Contact URL	☑ No Contact URL Availa
Screen Capture URL	

Letter | Campaign Letter ▾

Notes:

⊙ All contacts confirmed

Save   Pull Domain Info   Back

Figure 10-8. Rmoov Domain Editor

Site Speed

Site Speed is an important factor in SEO, and several tools are tailored to give you insight into your site's performance. Some of the tools include suggestions and reports that will help you analyze issues affecting page speed and determine any hindrances so your site can achieve optimal performance.

GTmetrix

GTmetrix helps you analyze the performance of your web pages. Google PageSpeed and Yahoo! YSlow rule sets are baked into the application. You can generate statistics such as the total page size and the number of requests for that site. You can also compare your site's speed with the average performance of sites analyzed on that platform. Generated visual and interactive reports, along with scheduled monitoring, make this a handy toolset for your SEO projects. This utility also passes your URLs through real-time Android devices to gauge performance on mobile platforms. Other features such as connection throttling and browser-based performance comparisons help you understand how your site performs at a high level. Figure 10-9 shows a sample report. More information on the toolset can be found at `https://gtmetrix.com`.

***Figure 10-9.** Sample report for the Google URL on GTmetrix*

DareBoost

DareBoost helps you diagnose and monitor the quality of your site using a web-based interface (see Figure 10-10). This is a no-frills toolkit that grills your website by taking it through 100 checkpoints including desktop and mobile testing. You can check your site's rendering speed and receive a list of suggestions that explain any issues in a nutshell. You can find more information at www.dareboost.com.

Figure 10-10. *DareBoost visual report*

Content Building and Optimization

User-engaging content is the driving factor in SEO; and, as you have heard a million times, *Content is king*. Various tools can help you build and optimize content.

Grammarly

Content displayed on your website should not have grammatical errors or incorrect words. Poor content can be a turn-off, especially when it is riddled with spelling and grammatical errors. Grammarly is a robust tool that can make a significant difference by helping to weed out grammatical and writing errors in your website content. You can also use it as a Google Chrome add-on. A built-in contextual spelling checker and context-optimized word suggestions result in content clarity and vocabulary enhancement, thereby improving readability significantly. Figure 10-11 shows the Grammarly tool. More information on this plug-in can be found at https://www.grammarly.com/.

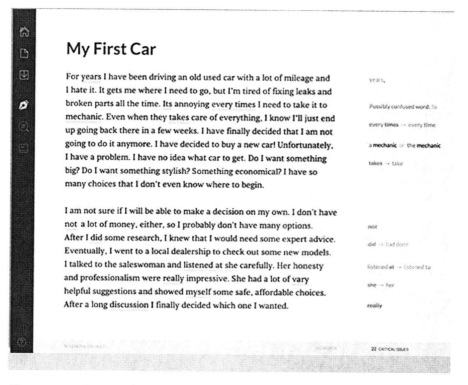

Figure 10-11. Grammarly

Siteliner

Siteliner is a tool that helps you find duplicate content in your domain and common content due to navigation, header, and footer issues. It helps you determine whether the content used is shallow and not unique, which may result in a bad UX. With features such as internal linking analysis and text-to-HTML ratio in addition to finding plagiarized content, this useful toolkit helps you gauge the viability of your content. Figure 10-12 shows the Siteliner user interface. More information can be found at www.siteliner.com/.

Explore your site.

[   ] **Go**

Find duplicate content, broken links, and more...

Figure 10-12. *Siteliner*

Hootsuite

Hootsuite is a social media management ecosystem. Content plays a relevant and significant role in your social media campaigns, so it is imperative that you have a tool to help you choose and categorize your content. Hootsuite also helps with content distribution and scheduling. You can find a comprehensive list of auto-generated conversation starters in your news feed (see Figure 10-13) and manage multiple content streams from social media networks such as Twitter, FourSquare, and LinkedIn. More information on this enterprise-grade toolkit can be found at `https://hootsuite.com/`.

Figure 10-13. *Hootsuite statistics*

BuzzSumo

The BuzzSumo platform helps you discover engaging content and provides you with content data that can be useful in your campaigns (see Figure 10-14). You can locate influencers and industry experts related to specific content categories. This tool also assists you in identifying trends and patterns related to your content in addition to providing a great deal of information via its content-research capabilities. You can analyze your competitors' content strategies and tactics using insight-driven competitive analysis. Alerts can be set up to keep you abreast of the latest developments, plus the tool provides domain comparison results. BuzzSumo is a tool that SEO and digital marketing experts must incorporate in social media campaigns and strategies. You can find more information at `http://buzzsumo.com/`.

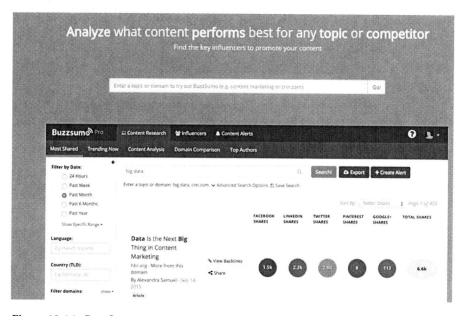

Figure 10-14. *BuzzSumo*

Site Audits

Several tools are available to perform a complete site checkup and list bottlenecks and problems. These audit tools can save you a lot of time and effort by pointing out the deficiencies of your site from an SEO perspective. It is impossible to check every factor manually. Plus, the factors change and may be rated higher or lower depending on the importance given to them by the search engines. You saw Screaming Frog's SEO Spider earlier in the chapter; it is a good audit tool that provides a panoptic view of your website's SEO needs. Let's look at some other efficient, popular tools that are widely used by SEO experts.

SEO SiteCheckup

SEO SiteCheckup performs a fast audit of your site and generates reports (see Figure 10-15). The suggestions and fixes are explained in a straightforward manner. You can check and compare the results for your site and your competitors (currently up to five competitors). The Professional Monitoring feature keep track of weekly alterations and auto-generates the latest SEO score for your site. More information about this utility can be found at http://seositecheckup.com/.

Figure 10-15. SEO Site Checkup

Once you enter a URL and click Checkup, a comprehensive report containing audit statistics is displayed, along with an SEO score. Figure 10-16 shows the output.

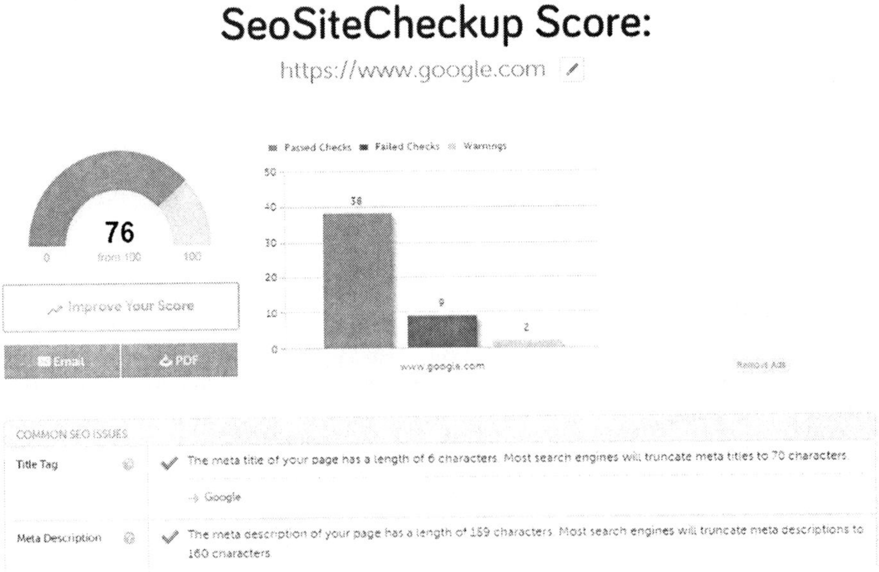

Figure 10-16. SEO Site Checkup report

In addition to performing a complete checkup, this site has many utilities to check factors manually including testing Robots.txt, sitemaps, favicons, doctype, and HTTPS.

WooRank

The WooRank tool performs a fast, comprehensive audit of your site and can detect and list on-page and off-page factors that are crucial to SEO success (see Figure 10-17). The SEO audit gives you a wide view of the mobile optimization and usability factors for your site. Complete with features that indicate crawl errors, localization, social media, and monitoring SERPs, this tool is used widely by SEO experts. Note that WooRank is a premium tool; you can learn more at www.woorank.com/.

Figure 10-17. WooRank SEO audit

Summary

There is no dearth of SEO tools on the market. SEO is a constantly changing methodology, so some tools become more popular as others lose their relevance. For example, you can find a suite of SEO tools on Moz at https://moz.com/tools. You can also use other prominent utilities such as SEO PowerSuite, SEMrush, HubSpot, Seoptimer, and Raven for SEO optimization and improvisation. The importance and relevance of SEO ranking factors are always changing, so there is no fixed rule that says you need to use a particular tool.

The next chapter gives you an overview of social media marketing and its relevance to SEO.

CHAPTER 11

■ ■ ■

Social Media Marketing and SEO

Social media marketing (SMM) is an integral part of SEO. In this era, social media is not just a basic factor you need to incorporate—it is a remarkable platform with a reach spanning more than 1 billion users. Current statistics indicate that Facebook is the leading social media platform with more than 1.5 billion users. In addition, there are Twitter, LinkedIn, and Foursquare, to name a few.

Earlier chapters emphasized the importance of providing user-engaging content to keep users interested in your website. But it is not just about content—social media is used as a hub for conversation and sharing.

Implementing SMM

Social media as a platform can no longer be neglected; it is a vital part of content marketing. For example, Facebook can be used as a means of understanding the behavior, preferences, and trends of young people who use it. LinkedIn is used for professional purposes including searching for potential employees and sharing updates about the latest products. But implementing SMM for SEO is not as straightforward as it may seem. You need to build an intuitive connection with your target audience to realize the potential of social media.

Following are some key aspects of how to use SEO-relevant social media to connect to a larger audience:

- Create brand-awareness and educate the target audience about your company's products and services. You can also nurture brand loyalty and develop trust and credibility with your consumer base by using social media advertising.

- Interact with current customers: connect with them via conversation and understand their viewpoint. Ask for feedback, and learn about their likes and dislikes; this will help you gain insight into your product's performance and shortcomings.

© Aravind Shenoy and Anirudh Prabhu 2016
A. Shenoy and A. Prabhu, *Introducing SEO*, DOI 10.1007/978-1-4842-1854-9_11

- Use game-changing content to keep users engaged and lure potential customers to your products. You will notice an increase in web traffic if you direct more people to your website leading, to higher ranking in the search engine results.

- Prompt users to share your content, to maximize the reach and scope of your projects.

- Use social media to introduce new products, promotions, and news. It helps if you have events coming up or if you want to share fresh information with your audience.

- Improve your marketing intelligence and make strategic decisions by understanding not only your products but also your business rivals. You can use media formats such as images, videos, and content to establish a media presence. You can track the results using analytics and use historical data to plan for the future and increase sales and revenue.

- Use localization techniques based on your business location, and target the audience in the vicinity. Learn about your consumer base and cultivate lead generation for people interested in your products and services.

- Use social media to distribute content such as blogs, whitepapers, and case studies. They will reach the audience more quickly and at a fraction of the cost compared to traditional marketing channels. Promoting product reviews and your company culture is beneficial in the long run. This is a good option for small- and medium-size businesses in particular, because they do not have the reach or advertising budget to target a huge customer base.

Popular Social Media Networks

There are many social media networks, as shown in Figure 11-1. This section gives you a brief overview on how to take advantage of the benefits offered by Facebook, LinkedIn, Google+, Yelp, Foursquare, Twitter, and Pinterest.

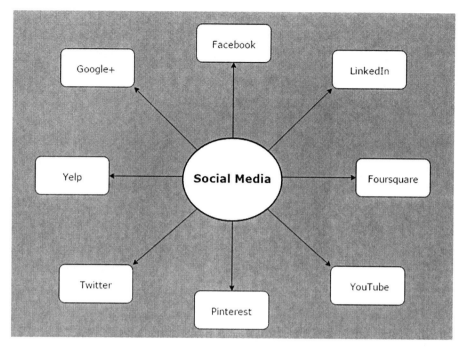

Figure 11-1. *Trendy social media portals*

Facebook

Facebook is the most popular social media platform and already has the largest consumer base; more than 1.5 billion people use Facebook in their day-to-day life. There are a number of ways to boost your online reputation using Facebook:

- Create Facebook pages for individual profiles and business pages for your organization.

- Use Facebook as a content distribution platform where you share updates and engage with your users. This leads to brand awareness and also helps customers be in sync with the latest news and promotions.

- Plan events and campaigns to reach out to a large audience and make customers an integral part of your setup.

- Spark lead generation and promote products to increase the span of business to potential customers.

- Use it as a platform for customer feedback and input. This helps you gain insight into customer preferences and marketing trends.

- Utilize community pages to involve users in corporate social responsibility and other tasks.

- Use the Facebook Ads service to cater to a specific group of consumers.

- Encourage users to like and share your product information. This can give a big boost to your online reputation in addition to lending credibility and trust to your products.

- Use the Facebook Places feature to keep your business partners, potential customers, and users abreast of your location. It allows users to check in on Facebook and spreads awareness of your business.

- Quality link building via blogs and web pages will lead to increased traffic and make your site more visible. This is an organic way of connecting with your target audience. You can also keep users engaged by using quality content, which will increase your rankings—relevant content is a vital cog in content-marketing wheel.

- Link your Facebook pages with other social media platforms, and reach out to a wider audience

- Advertise your products and goods for a fraction of the cost compared to traditional marketing methods, and enhance the user experience with engaging content. The analytics for your page will provide insight into customer trends and preferences in addition to conversion optimization.

LinkedIn

LinkedIn is one of the most sought-after professional social networking sites when it comes to business. It is an excellent platform for entrepreneurs and business owners to showcase their services.

Following are some ways you can get the most from LinkedIn:

- Showcase your products and services by using the company page to cater to your target audience.

- Interact with potential customers to accumulate a larger user base and generate leads for your projects.

- Implementing quality link building to direct more users to your web page and increase traffic

- Advertise your products and share regular updates with your connections and others in the industry.

- Create groups and connect with relevant people in the industry via second- and third-degree connections, thereby expanding the scope of your business. Collaborate with industry experts, especially those in business-to-business (B2B), and keep them updated about your services by using feeds and updates.

- Use relevant, quality content to keep your audience in sync with the latest developments.

- Spot and hire talent using LinkedIn profiles, especially those with experience in your domain.

- Use ad campaigns to promote your products and create brand awareness.

- Get recommendations for your businesses from professionals and subject matter experts, thus creating trust and credibility.

- Use commercial utilities such as LinkedIn Premium for detailed information about B2B, potential job seekers, and statistics to update your strategies.

Google+

Google+ is another social media platform that can help extend the scope of your business. You can use the various toolkits Google has in its arsenal to take your business to the next level.

You can optimize your online reputation by using the following tactics on Google+:

- Google My Business is a great utility that enables customers to reach out to your business whenever they search or use Google+ to locate you. Create a Google My Business account, and link Google Maps to it using the API. You can start conversations with your consumer base and respond to customer feedback using this toolkit. Localization is an important SEO factor and helps small- and medium-size business enhance their scope in their vicinity.

- You can use the built-in Embedded Posts feature and intuitive media such as images, videos, and text links to ensure visibility for your posts.

- Google includes the Google Badge feature, which lets customers find and preview a community before eventually joining it. Such ventures are good for corporate social responsibility and campaigns.

- Google's AdWords and pay-per-click utilities can help you gain ground by directly placing your site at the top of search results. This will result in better online sales and ensure visibility on SERPs (although it is not an organic approach).

- Google Hangouts enables instant messaging, video and voice chat, and VOIP features using your Google+ account. For example, you can simplify your video conferencing needs using Google Hangouts.

- Create a Google+ community +to cater to a wide audience. You can also create social media contests and campaigns using the platform. Other utilities include Blogger to create blogs and Drive to store data and documents on a large scale.

- Gain insight into your commercial projects by networking via the Google+ platform and using analytics tools to understand market trends and statistics. You can rework your marketing strategies in response to the reports and boost your project visibility in Google search results.

Twitter

Twitter is a micro-blogging platform that currently has more than 300 million users. It allows you to post tweets—short messages, limited to 140 characters—making it compatible with SMS. Twitter can be used in a various ways, including to promote products and share news with a large audience.

Following are some ways you can enhance your business flow with Twitter:

- Use Twitter as a content distribution platform by sharing links to your blog or other social networking platforms such as Reddit where you have posted relevant content.

- Get feedback from customers by using Twitter as it is a channel for instant input. Revise your customer relationship strategies and rework your tactics in response to comments from users. For example, if you post about a product, you may receive feedback about its strengths and weaknesses or services related to the product. This gives you an opportunity to make changes and improve your goods.

- Increase awareness of your brand and get recommendations from a wide audience for recent launches. Even celebrities use Twitter to share their views with clients and fans. Engage your users with short messages and cater to various groups using direct messages in addition to public tweeting.

- Spot and hire talented employees by reaching out to as many people as possible when you have a vacant position in your company. You can also use Twitter to send internal messages to your team even if they are geographically separated. Twitter's reach is significant, and it is an excellent means for promoting your services. Make it a referral engine by submitting and receiving recommendations about clients, groups, or the entire community.

Pinterest

Engaging users with visual media is the most important part of SEO in this era. For industries such as journalism and fashion, visual media is the norm. You can use Pinterest in several ways to promote your product; studies related to digital marketing suggest an increase in popularity and sales in response to the use of interactive visual media such as images and infographics. (Seeing is believing!)

You can use Pinterest in your SEO and social media marketing projects using the following options:

- Use infographics and relevant pictures as pins to engage with your customers and potential leads.

- Use Pinterest's commercial features to promote your products, and use the analytics tool to gain insight into customer preferences, sales conversions, and bounce rates.

- Link to other social media platforms such as Quora and Twitter to extend the scope of your business. Also, share your views and recommendations for other boards. At the same time, keep your board updated with multiple pins to create interest and build professional relationships with other users and potential clients.

- Create boards for your employees and potential customers with photos of team meetings and business deals. Share graphics of customer experiences as pinned images to create good rapport with your user base. Use relevant keywords in the titles and descriptions of your boards to make optimal use of your account.

- You can pin videos from Vimeo and YouTube to promote products. Visually intuitive media is an integral part of SEO strategies, because search engines rate user interaction and engagement highly.

- Make your pins user friendly by using Place Pins that let you pin images with maps. This is extremely useful in the tourism industry, because you can view pictures of shopping locations, hotels, and public places.

YouTube

YouTube may not be your favorite social networking site, but it is an excellent platform for connecting with your audience. There are various ways you can use YouTube to promote products and services:

- Create tutorials, lectures, and online training for your users.

- Use promotional videos to reach out to customers. Include do-it-yourself projects to further educate your customers about how to work with products and services.

- Use YouTube's commercial advertising platform to create and publish ads.

- Integrate with its parent Google+ account to cater to a wide audience.

- Post quality links to your website or blogs, and keep user interest alive with regular updates and comments.

Yelp

Yelp is a handy utility for small- and medium-size businesses that do not have the budget for traditional advertising and are looking to expand their local business in a particular location.

You can use Yelp to boost your business by implementing the following steps:

- Pay close attention to customer reviews. Understand the needs of the customer and also look for ways to expand your customer base by learning about the requirements of prospective customers. Responding to customers' needs demonstrates genuine empathy and concern. Customer feedback and reviews are important for local businesses to survive in a highly competitive market.

- Analyze the business graph and check traffic from customers in your vicinity. Track your progress and optimize your strategy by using the built-in metrics.

- Include interactive media such as images and photos, and use specific keywords to describe your product.

- Offer special promotions, deals, and offers to customers to increase online sales. For example, post a list of coupon codes that offer discounts on various products, especially during the Christmas season, to help develop a reliable customer base.

Foursquare

Foursquare is a geotechnology social networking service catering to mobile users. It can help you discover and share information about the businesses and organizations around you. You can check in whenever you visit a commercial establishment. Because Foursquare's geotechnology is used by other social media platforms such as Vine and Flickr, you can plan strategies to get the maximum benefit from this platform.

You can use Foursquare to improve your local business in the following ways:

- Understand customers' likes and dislikes by analyzing reviews and comments.

- Develop a relationship with users by using trivia and contests.

- Offers, deals, and badges can be used as promotional materials for your business. Offer discounts to customers who have gained perks and badges using Foursquare; this creates a positive customer experience and can increases your online reputation.

- Post tips and use Foursquare's ad services to extend your reach in the vicinity.

With mobile telephony gaining momentum and becoming the prime channel for e-commerce, the number of social media apps is increasing by the day—the list seems endless. For example, in addition to the other sites discussed here, Instagram is an image- and video-based social media application that is hugely popular and trendy.

Social bookmarking sites are evolving and play a major role in SEO-related social media marketing. (*Social bookmarking sites* are centralized online services where users save links to web pages that they intend to share.) For example, Pinterest, Flickr and Reddit are popular and widely-used social bookmarking sites catering to a large audience. You can access the bookmarks through any computer that provides access to the internet. You can share links with your connections and also sneak a peek at links that other users tag on the platform. Using these sites, you can drive traffic and valuable backlinks to your site. Social bookmarking is SEO-centric in that you can introduce a website or web page to the search engines before the crawlers locate the web page through inbound links. External metadata using relevant keywords, categorization, and hits improves the SEO profile for the site or web page.

Summary

Social media marketing is an integral part of SEO. You need to post regular updates and interact with your target audience on a regular basis. Organizing and sharing interesting content will boost your SEO process and deliver results in the long term. Search engines and their spiders are getting smarter, and it can be complicated to try to connect with your customers and leads globally. Using modern marketing practices, you can increase your online sales and drive traffic to your site.

You don't need to go overboard and create personal and business profiles on every social media platform; the right mix of profiles and quality content are the key factors that will enhance your customers' experience. Remember, social media with SEO should not be search engine centric but must focus on user intent and requirements. Using the many available analytics tools, you can identify shortcomings and roadblocks, rework business-critical decisions, and predict future trends. The roadmap is complex but leads to an optimal user experience.

Index

© Aravind Shenoy and Anirudh Prabhu 2016
A. Shenoy and A. Prabhu, *Introducing SEO*, DOI 10.1007/978-1-4842-1854-9

Get the eBook for only $5!

Why limit yourself?

Now you can take the weightless companion with you wherever you go and access your content on your PC, phone, tablet, or reader.

Since you've purchased this print book, we're happy to offer you the eBook in all 3 formats for just $5.

Convenient and fully searchable, the PDF version enables you to easily find and copy code—or perform examples by quickly toggling between instructions and applications. The MOBI format is ideal for your Kindle, while the ePUB can be utilized on a variety of mobile devices.

To learn more, go to www.apress.com/companion or contact support@apress.com.

Apress®
THE EXPERT'S VOICE™

CPSIA information can be obtained
at www.ICGtesting.com
Printed in the USA
FFOW01n1326151216
30449FF